The Paradigm of Harmonious Progress in Energy

The Paradigm of Harmonious Progress in Energy

By

Valentinas Klevas and Audrone Klevienė

Cambridge
Scholars
Publishing

The Paradigm of Harmonious Progress in Energy

By Valentinas Klevas and Audrone Klevienė

This book first published 2020

Cambridge Scholars Publishing

Lady Stephenson Library, Newcastle upon Tyne, NE6 2PA, UK

British Library Cataloguing in Publication Data
A catalogue record for this book is available from the British Library

ISBN (10): 1-5275-5433-3
ISBN (13): 978-1-5275-5433-7

TABLE OF CONTENTS

LIST OF FIGURES

LIST OF TABLES

FOREWORD

"My theory lacks facts", said Holmes.

(From Arthur Conan Doyle's "The Casebook of Sherlock Holmes".)

There is no shortage of facts, both positive and negative, to formulate the theoretical principles of harmonious progress in energy. There is a lack of an essential principle, namely an emphasis on the root causes of such uncontrolled destruction of nature, a generalisation of these assumptions, and, in particular, a broad approach that would provide meaningful insights. Evaluation of the current state is still being left to one side when considering economic issues. In other words, there is a lack of insight when discussing what the harmonious balance between human activity and nature means and why it still has not been achieved. Therefore, the motto of this study is an excerpt from A. Šliogeris' preface to Schelling's Philosophical Investigations into the Essence of Human Freedom:

> Schelling was not concerned with the conquering of nature and technical violation, but with the harmonious balance between man and nature; harmony between a human and his origin is of the utmost importance when the human soul does not lose its naturalness, and nature pulsates with the rhythm of the soul.

There is deep wisdom in this phrase: on the one hand, man feels part of nature and, on the other hand, assumes the great mission of spiritualising nature without, of course, denying the laws of improvement, as stated by the Eternal Creator.

First of all, it is necessary to answer the question regarding why I intend to undertake such a difficult, albeit seemingly already being solved, and "polished" task—to substantially revise the concept of sustainable energy development, which conveys the idea of energy progress. However, I want to clarify in advance that in this work, I not only reinterpret the notion of sustainable energy development (currently, it's too narrow category) but present it as a paradigm of harmonious progress in energy, which, in its essence, is not the same. In the social sciences, the essence of the paradigm is the totality of assumptions, concepts, values and activities that reflect the worldview and perception of reality within a given community. The concept of sustainable energy development does not have sufficient dynamics and economic viability for implementation. It should be noted that the concept of sustainable development has almost no connection with that particular content, expressing the global nature of the threats and, at the same time, links with the human mentality, which precisely create the problems. I note one important statement—as a result of constant repetition, it seems to be *a priori* correct, that it is “us” who are responsible for this devastation. However, this is a fundamental mistake, since it does not name who those “us” are, nor does it make it clear on what ideological, and, therefore, legal basis this ominous, supposedly unmanageable devastation is taking place. There has been a fundamental mistake in people’s minds that justifies the inability of economic theory and economic activity to prevent the destruction of nature, and the origin of this mistake is a depiction of human progress—unrestricted economic growth, the main criterion of which is continuous Gross Domestic Product (GDP) growth. Nature is being sacrificed to this endeavour and it is considered an inevitable necessity. Basing their opinion on some kind of fantastic anthropocentric law, humans have decided that nature is a warehouse, the contents of which must be freely used, and it is nature’s responsibility to deal with pollution caused by economic activities. The whole economic mechanism is created precisely based on this anthropocentric worldview. However, activities based on this point of view are experiencing serious and ever-increasing reactions of nature, affecting not only humans but all vegetation and life in general, which is the foundation of human existence. The obvious protests regarding climate change and its consequences—catastrophes—were briefly summarised by Prof. R. Čiegis when he stated that nature will never adapt to the indiscriminate needs of man. Instead, man will have to conform to nature without destructing its laws which have been evolving for millions of years.

The unbridled pursuit of profits is based on a strangely impaired and insanely promoted propensity to consume, in particular, the development of consumption opportunities, considered as an indicator of human well-being.

The paradigm of harmonious progress is based on the humanist worldview that defines nature and its laws, influencing human life, as the main foundation of human existence. According to humanists, nature is the main pillar of human life, therefore, from the economic point of view, nature and all life has to be considered with huge respect, and viewed as an essential value, not as an inexhaustible source of wealth which can be recklessly exploited.

From the dynamic point of view, the dimension of harmony means that the process is not being ignored and is being corrected according to all the related aspects in the long-term perspective. Energetics is a branch of economics, the functioning of which is essential for the development of the economy and causes the most difficult, poorly theoretically defined and practically estimated issues—reliability of the energy supply, environmental protection and quality of renewability. Theoretical and practical evaluation of these aspects is essential; therefore, it is being increasingly discussed, seeking to provide the meaning for harmonious development in energy and to substantiate its contents.

Harmonious progress declares advancement based on deep ecology, which stands for the reversible process, whereas technological progress is based on renewable energy sources and energy preservation as an alternative for energy consumption when due to the use of smart technologies, energy consumers can also become energy providers. This requires a wide and well-structured knowledge of the natural and social processes, which results in harmonious progress and its evaluation.

Thus, this discussion raises questions that will be answered in this study, namely: a) Who is responsible for the devastation of nature and on what theoretical and legal basis—this is a crucial issue for the dominant paradigm; b) What the progress is, and whether or not the nature conservation process can be managed, in other words, whether it can be stopped by intelligent human action, and not merely by a fragmentary response to natural anomalies and catastrophes caused by climate change; c) What is considered as progress in a narrower field of life—energetics—which can and must play the avant-garde role in progress as the burning of fossil fuels and their products in energy and transport, in particular, is already widely identified as the main culprit in climate change.

Many years of experience and intense insight into the problem allow me to think that I have the right and even the duty to fulfil my mission as a scientist: to fundamentally clarify the essence of the problem in dynamics, defining the root causes, looking back to the past, and anticipating the guidelines, or at least a vision for the future.

Concluding this brief introduction, I would like to express my gratitude to Audrone Klevienė, junior research associate at the Lithuanian Energy Institute Laboratory for Renewable Energy and Energy Efficiency, who is essentially the co-author of this monograph, since the whole of Chapter Two, and the analysis of the knowledge economy, in general, is based on her work.

Finally, it is important to add that the evolving concept of the knowledge economy has crystallised the structural elements of knowledge itself. Much of the knowledge is not derived from the individual efforts of our generation but is gained from past generations. Thus, knowledge is, by its very nature, a public good, the supply of which is not diminished when it is transmitted to another person. Therefore, this monograph also aspires to the status of a public good in the hope that it will serve the advancement of science.

PART I

THEORETICAL OUTLINE OF THE HARMONIOUS PROGRESS PARADIGM

CHAPTER ONE

ANALYSIS OF DIFFERENCES IN PARADIGMS OF PROGRESS AND HARMONIOUS PROGRESS: CHARACTERISTICS OF THE PROBLEM IN LITERARY SOURCES

The concept of the paradigm. The essential attitude of the dominant paradigm in the interaction between nature and man

First of all, one has to characterise in more detail the specificity and meaning of the term "paradigm". In the social sciences, the essence of the paradigm is the totality of assumptions, concepts, values and activities that reflect the worldview and perception of reality in a given community.

To give meaning to the emerging paradigm of harmonious progress, it is necessary to diagnose the origins and consequences of the existing paradigm, its shortcomings, or at least its insufficiencies. However, it is first and foremost a matter of defining the meaning of this category; otherwise, it will be difficult to understand why the term paradigm is used rather than theory, concept or methodology.

In terms of the concept of paradigm and its content, the contribution of T. S. Kuhn is paramount (Andersen, Barker and Chen 2003). T. S. Kuhn claims that theories, laws and concepts cannot function by themselves. They become meaningful only in the paradigm in which they occur, and the paradigm is also a philosophical-social category. In this work, it is necessary to state the already known truth that philosophical systems and insights are far more influential than imagined even in these times of scientific specialisation. T. S. Kuhn has analysed science from a historical point of view, in contrast to K. R. Popper, who begins the analysis and evaluation from a very late period of science (Popper 1959), one which already has a wealth of theories that can be compared to one another and tested by experiment. According to T. S. Kuhn, the paradigm can function without any theory. The paradigm is pre-theoretical.

A theory is a much later and paradigm-dependent phenomenon. Without it, science would not be able to progress, or at least, progress would be slow. The paradigm allows researchers to expand their knowledge faster without having to re-prove their underlying assumptions. Often, there are underlying implications, and the primary origins only appear when problems arise. "When an individual scholar can adopt a paradigm without proof, he no longer has to try to reconstruct his field of work starting from the original principles and justifying the use of each new concept" (Kuhn 1970).

Paradigm is a much broader term than theory because it encompasses an entire worldview or ideology. If these tools become inadequate, the emergence of new tools aimed at solving the problems more efficiently may lead to a new paradigm. But a paradigm can also be changed by painful events, such as ecological and economic crises, which has happened many times, but the essential paradigm of the interaction between humans and nature has not changed from the New Times and the teachings of Descartes, who might be named the initiator of the epoch, based on science and mathematics, as the arbiter of absolute truth. In this paradigm, nature is considered to be an inexhaustible source of physical resources and an infinite absorber of by-products of the production processes. It is believed that environmental damage will always be repaired if necessary. As Schelling put it, "The common flaw of the modern European philosophy (starting with Descartes) is that for it, nature does not exist and has no viable foundation" (Schelling 1995). Particular emphasis should be placed on the remoteness of urban residents from nature. The view of the relationship between society and nature "is based on a vision of unrestricted growth as the progress of humanity. According to this perspective, technological development is aimed at increasing the power of socio-economic systems, increasing production and using the environment to accumulate negative effects. Encouraged by technical progress, in practice, the technocratic paradigm has increasingly displaced the humanist and environmental paradigm" (Čiegis 2002).

Therefore, one of the major obstacles to progress might be the fact that people's mentality has changed fundamentally in a historically short time. The rapid flow of technology is creating an artificial world, pushing society away from nature. The Lithuanian philosopher, A. Maceina (2004) wrote:

> The cultural world and cultural life do not stand on the natural world and natural life as a palace on the foundation. [...] Nature is disappearing from our horizons. It begins to exist not as nature, but only as the material basis of the new world.

According to the discussion of the concept of the paradigm of harmonious progress in energy, it is necessary to elaborate its content (basic principles) and consequences, and finally to link it with the concept of the sustainable development of energy. Given the current state of the global economy, the ecological crisis and the real steps towards a global agreement in 2015 concerning the measures to prevent the catastrophic consequences of climate change, we must point out that the underlying contradictions remain in the basic paradigmatic assumptions that no one doubts anymore. The basic paradigm that has dominated for several centuries regarding the interaction between the economic activity of humanity and nature remains unchanged. What is worse is that the concept of progress is identified with the pursuit of economic progress, while the individual and his life goals remain within the frame of the economic man (*homo economicus*). And this is undoubtedly a major obstacle as regards progress.

In this work, we declare that the paradigm of harmonious progress is based on a worldview which, in short, recognises nature, including the laws which govern man, as the determining power for humanity's existence. I refer to the great humanists who created the philosophy of the meaning of human life and its human purpose, which views nature as the basis of human beings and existence. Economic progress is closely linked to great respect for nature as an intrinsic value, not just an inexhaustible wealth of resources that can be recklessly exploited.

Problems of the formation of the paradigm of harmonious progress of energy in the context of the sustainable development doctrine

According to the general concept, the notion of harmonious progress must have a link with the concept of sustainable development, which was formulated in the relatively recent time of 1987. The Doctrine of Sustainable Development, formulated in 1987 and published in the Brundtland Commission report "Our Common Future", clearly represents nature's response to unprecedented levels of pollution and resource over-exploitation in history, causing the devastating effects of climate change, as well as the uneven economic development of individual countries. But this currently exceptionally fashionable term—sustainable development—is manipulated by constant new insights and attributes. It has become a sort of obsession, blocking the progress and advancement of thought. I will explain this situation briefly.

Sustainable development is increasingly being presented as a pathway to all that is good and desirable in society. Some of the proposed national indicators of sustainable development from the United States, the United Kingdom, and Finland illustrate this point. They include such factors as crime rate; participation of 14-year-olds in social organisational work; teacher capabilities; workforce skill level; classes taught in a minority language; children in public care; number of smokers; internet users; how children get to school; obesity rates; and R&D expenditures, etc. (Banister 2008); (Holden 2007); (Holden and Linnerud 2007). Unquestionably, sustainable development is still an important concept, which was clearly illustrated at the United Nations Conference on Sustainable Development (Rio+20), held in Rio de Janeiro in June 2012. One of the conference's main outcomes was the agreement by member states to set up sustainable development goals, which could be useful tools in achieving sustainable development. Thus, achieving sustainable development is still high on the international and national agendas 25 years after the concept was launched with the publication of "Our Common Future", commonly referred to as the Brundtland report. According to the World Commission on Environment and Development (WCED):

> Even though there is not yet any political or scientific agreement on a definition of sustainable development, it remains remarkably persistent as an ideal political concept, similar to democracy, justice, and liberty (Meadowcroft 2007). Indeed, sustainable development is now like "democracy": it is universally desired, diversely understood, extremely difficult to achieve, and won't go away (Lafferty 2004).

In other words, additions to the definition of sustainable energy development, and its enrichment with various nuances, are virtually useless. Although there have already been endless additions to the definition of sustainable development, the list grows longer yearly. Thus, the concept of sustainable development has become so comprehensive and complex that it is no longer useful in guiding policymaking. Not surprisingly, many scholars have argued that the sustainable development concept is in danger of becoming irrelevant e.g. (Hopwood, Mellor and O'Brien 2005); (Redclift 2005). In support of this view, one has to agree that the concept of sustainable development must acquire a clear and coherent direction and the prerequisites for achieving a common goal. To expect real progress, there is a need to distinguish between essential aspects that must inspire fundamental paradigmatic attitudes, and, in the case of our planet's situation, the quest to save nature, in regards of which all other aspirations based on various indicators are expressed. Time is running out, therefore, it is necessary to act, instead of working on new definitions. The key point, summarising the above statements, is that the concept/theory of sustainable energy development is based on the old paradigm. The Brundtland report did not set a taboo concerning nature, which means that the basic paradigm approach to the unbridled exploitation of nature has remained, which is precisely what leads to a dead end. Any attempt to implement a noble idea of sustainable development is undermined by the notion of economic advancement. Economic growth has remained an essential goal in almost all countries, and it is officially proclaimed as an infallible panacea for resolving all hardships. Without a basic paradigmatic approach to nature conservation, the relentless pursuit of economic growth beyond natural boundaries will not help to achieve the goals of sustainable development. Sustainable development remains a slogan without real content. Therefore, the concept of sustainable development needs to be fundamentally replaced by the concept and content of the paradigm of harmonious progress in nature conservation and regeneration. At the same time, it is a plan for the salvation of all life and humanity. Bearing in mind that in social sciences, the essence of the paradigm is the totality of assumptions, concepts, values and activities that reflect the worldview and perception of reality in a given community, it can be stated that it is also an aspiration of the progress of life in general, and the directions of this path can be called a methodology.

In energetics, the concept of limited development has existed since the global oil crisis in 1973, in dissonance with the dominant concept of economic progress. First of all, the main difference is that the end-user, in favour of which the production process is happening, has to dispose of the used goods, including food waste, into the environment (landfill) at the end of the product's life cycle or, simply, if so decided by the consumer. Characterising the contemporary economic trends, I quote the statement from Bauman's book, "Culture in Fluid Modernity":

> Shifting the emphasis from possession to disposal, elimination, and discarding is perfectly in line with the logic of a consumer-oriented economy. People clinging to yesterday's clothing, computers and mobile phones can bring disaster to an economy, whose primary concern and *sine qua non* of survival is the rapid and accelerating disposal of purchased goods into landfill (Bauman, 2015).

While energy is being fully consumed, this is defined by physical law. In other words, the nature of the commodity is fundamentally different and, for decades, the aim has been to reduce energy consumption and increase energy efficiency. This will be discussed in more detail in other chapters. The unique property of energy, as a commodity, is the ability to express all forms of energy at any stage of production, transformation and end-use in specific units—J (joules), kWh (kilowatt-hours), toe (tonnes of oil equivalent).

Therefore, if the dominant economic theory is that growth, which is considered equal to advancement, is driven by consumption at the highest possible level, and is directed at the mass consumption of things, including unnecessary and surplus items, then, in energetics, it is already clearly recognised that for energy growth (and not just growth), the inevitable alternative is energy conservation, which is understood as saving energy (at the end-use stage) and increasing energy efficiency (at the energy transformation stage). Bearing in mind the enormous amounts of energy consumed that can be reduced not only through direct savings, but also by home renovation and increasing energy efficiency, I introduced the concept of energy conservation (Klevas 1998). In my later works, I developed this concept further (Klevas 2015).

However, the most important problem that forms the core of the solution to the problems of harmonious progress is that waste—including waste in the form of harmful emissions causing climate change—is generated during the process of transforming (burning) fossil energy, especially in transport. Therefore, the most important emphasis in attempting to define the paradigm of harmonious advancement in energy is the breakdown of energy resources into fossil fuels produced over millions of years by natural evolution (e.g. coal, oil and natural gas) and renewable energy sources (solar, wind and environmental, etc.), that do not pollute the environment. In the last decade, the development of renewable energy sources has become a major trend in the development of energetics. The long-term goals of the individual energetics strategies of Europe, especially Denmark and Germany (Hansen, Mathiesen and Skov 2019), of replacing burning fossil fuels with renewable energy by almost 100%, is stunning in terms of innovation and courage. During this period, other countries, including Lithuania, have also been embarking on this path, declaring a strategic target of up to 80 per cent of the use of renewable energy sources by 2050. However, it should be noted that northern European countries have been preparing for this for a long time—politically, scientifically and practically (technologically)—in terms of infrastructure construction for almost five decades since the oil crisis of 1973, and after the shock caused by it in the entire industrial world. But most importantly, and above all, these countries have laid the foundation for reshaping people's mentality in their countries, which is inevitable for the creation of a new type of energetics (Broto and Bulkeley 2013). Basically, that means switching to efficient energy consumption and replacing fossil fuels with renewable energy sources.

Not by coincidence, according to the happiness index which has been published since 2012 on the Solutions Network of the United Nations, and covers 156 countries, Northern European countries are leading: Finland (for the second year in a row), Denmark, Norway and Iceland. The list is established based on various factors: per capita GDP, data on population health and access to medical services, social benefits, civil rights and the prevalence of corruption (Castells and Himanen 2002).

The residents of Finland simply cannot be unhealthy due to the number of forests, covering 60 per cent of the country's land, which determines the purity of the air. Also, almost every second family has a sauna, which shows their extraordinary need for cleanliness and hygiene. Even having these huge areas of forests, they choose to preserve them and do not clear cut them but use a technique that allows selective logging instead. Countries, such as the Netherlands and Switzerland, where environmentalism prevails over the greedy profit interest, also rank high. Meanwhile, in countries where there is a greater amount of greed and a lower level of intelligence, the situation is the opposite (Routti and Yla-Anttila 2005).

In the concept of the paradigm, there is also a totality of assumptions as regards the realisation of the aspiration that manifests itself in the content and comprehensiveness of preparation. Namely, it is the dynamism of the implementation of harmonious progress. In other words, it is a methodology that covers the theoretical tools, organisational assumptions and methods. An example could be the mere fact that masses of modern renewable energy sources (RES) are being deployed in the use of smart grids, essentially turning ordinary energy consumers into consuming manufacturers. This process requires an intense teaching procedure, not only to change the mentality of the people but also to prepare the next generation of professionals. Economic incentives alone are far from able to make this process happen. It requires big organisational and technological improvements, ensuring adequate funding for revolutionary administrative reforms. In terms of the implementation of the Lithuanian Energy Strategy, by 2023, the Energy Service Organisation (ESO) plans to purchase and equip approximately 1.6 million remote-controlled power smart meters for all electricity consumers in the country—from the smallest to the largest. Although the tender has not yet been announced, the company estimates that the value of the project of smart accounting implementation in Lithuania could reach more than 200 million euros. Also, bearing in mind that the use of RES technologies is an essential tool to reduce emissions, which is critical to preventing climate change, it can be argued that energetics, based on RES technologies, is potentially penetrating all spheres of economics. Recently, northern European countries have prepared a programme to meet climate change commitments. In this programme, the dominant theme is the introduction of RES technologies (Nordic Council of Ministers 2019). Among the defined measures, significant importance is placed on the reforestation programme.

Therefore, the transformation of energy from exhaustive fossil fuels, causing enormous pollution, to RES, is considered an expression of the progress of life in general, as this process no longer contradicts the fundamental laws of nature which seem to be disappearing from the horizon of human life due to the incredible advancement of technology. Sadly, it seems to be lost from the perspective of scientists as well. This means that a change in people's mentality is crucial for success, and the most important element in terms of energetics would be the understanding of the importance of RES. This is particularly noticeable in cities. That is why, when it comes to progress, one has to look back at the philosophical reflections of humans as the apex of the evolutionary process of nature, to which thousands of years of philosophers' efforts have been devoted.

The concept of progress and the necessity of its transformation

If the term "harmonious" means a connection with nature, then the essence of the concept of advancement remains the fundamental problem, since it contains extremely broad content. The notion of progress has captivated people, especially those living in Western countries, for centuries. In his monograph, Professor Čiegis aptly stated: "Probably, speaking in general, no concept was as important to the Western world as the idea of progress and the belief in the continuous improvement of imperfect humanity. But the modern world is increasingly losing the momentum of real progress, as the thinkers of the enlightened age understood it, and is far from being in harmony with nature" (Čiegis 1997).

The Lithuanian philosopher, A. Maceina stated:

> Half of the nineteenth century was enslaved by the so-called theory of evolution, the origins of which were published by Darwin and Lamarck. In various forms, this theory has been repeated by various scholars: it has been modified, supplemented, criticized and corrected. Today, in its primal form, evolutionism no longer exists. The mechanical and materialistic basis of it is completely demolished. Today, no one dares to proclaim that the development of beings is driven by the struggle for survival or adaptation to the environment. Today, natural science proponents are observing the evolutionary pattern of the living world, a kind of plan executed by living and purposeful forces of nature. There is a certain grand, pre-determined and

defined plan of nature, and living life is not stagnant in its kinds and forms (Maceina 2004).

But you must have in mind that the basis of life is the Earth, climate, atmosphere, air purity, and many other phenomena to which human activities pose a threat. According to Prof. J. Brėdikis:

> The driving force behind evolution is far from Darwin's premise of the "eternal struggle for existence", and the struggle of the species for survival and natural selection, when the strongest wins. That power is the programmed survival of those who can adapt, unite and collaborate. Darwin's view is unacceptable simply because, according to his point of view, the struggle for survival is inevitable not only for wildlife but also for nations, races and states (Brėdikis 2015).

The problem, however, is that evolutionary theory is not being related to humans' relationship with nature and its laws.

In modern society, especially in the Western world, progress is, unfortunately, in many cases perceived as technological advancement and economic growth, whose ideological basis lies in the supposedly free market glorified by Smith, the effectiveness of which was linked to the liberation from any legal or other restrictions in the 19th and 20th centuries (Smith 1999); (Friedman 1998). Even after the Brundtland Commission report of 1987, the debate has continued with fierce attacks on those who, from their point of view, try to put the halter on the free market (Beckerman 1994). However, it is gradually becoming clear, even without specific proof, that the free market is the free exploitation of nature and, indeed, of people. The concept of progress and its content are still relevant globally, especially to Western society, but the problem is that there is a need to correct the meaning of the concept of progress that has become evident due to the errors in economic theory. The concept of progress has undergone a significant historical transformation in a very short time. The achievements of the sciences, especially the applied ones, and their very practical military applications have shaken the consciousness of humanity to the point of losing the concept of evolution as a law of progress. The belief that human evolution has reached its peak and has nothing to do with the evolution of nature has come into being. Instead of the advancement of species, there is a decline of species at an unprecedented rate. The predominance of technology in life has created an artificial sphere of life that is supposedly independent of nature, where progress is considered in isolation from the powerful laws of evolution, though, in fact, they are the fundamental laws of progress. The scale of technological innovation is impressive and causes fascination with the progress that is supposedly taking over the evolutionary relay. But the threatening reaction of nature to this direction of "evolution" shows that those authors who declare the need to find a way out of the dead end, in one way or another, are completely right. There has not been such technological progress in terms of advancement and pace, although ancient scientific achievements are also surprising in some respects. However, is the concept of progress correctly treated? The problem is that the concept of technological advancement has been consecrated to such an extent that no one in the Western world is resisting the penetration of this idea into all spheres of life. Even worse is that "Progress is first and foremost considered to be an unstoppable process that takes place independently of our desires and regardless of our feelings—a process in which victorious power requires our humble obedience" (Bauman 2015). Indeed, modern society blindly relies on self-advancement, which, unfortunately, is almost merged with the growth of the economy in terms of GDP, achieved through the progress of technological advancement and its implementation.

Many authors also note the parallel decline in attention and funding for basic sciences in favour of applied science (Teilhard de Chardin 1995).

However, natural disasters, recognised by the scientific world as a consequence of CO_2 emissions caused by fossil fuel combustion, make even the most short-sighted optimists think about the direction in which technological progress is developing. The balance of nature, achieved through millions of years of evolution, has been seriously disturbed in the last century alone. This is an undeniable proof of the "breakthrough" in applied science. What is more, this fact is already acknowledged not only by scientists, but also by global politics: at the end of 2015, countries of the world succeeded in signing the Paris Agreement on Climate Change, which demonstrates the global importance of the problem, but this is only the beginning of major changes in economic and, especially, energy policy for most countries. Never before has there been such a unanimous decision on any other issue. Unfortunately, relapses are also possible, as shown by the US withdrawal from this treaty. However, the fact that the treaty has been signed by almost all countries of the world proves that the burning of fossil fuels and their products in the energy and transport sectors is identified as the main cause of climate change. Agreements have been made as regards the indicators, but not on how these indicators could be pursued in the context of the mass Western level of consumption. It is unanimously acknowledged that the most important direction of energy development is the mass utilisation of renewable energy technologies, however, fierce resistance, including an ideological-methodological one, has arisen and is still going on. What's more, there are new, extremely threatening phenomena that are being built on the foundations of the lobbying industry. The major one among them is deforestation in many parts of the world. Paradoxically, in the spotlight of the apotheosis of biofuels, or, indeed, mass deforestation in Europe, in Lithuania, the incentive to use renewable fuels is taking place on a huge scale. The mere fact of a numerical indication of RES does not mean that progress is being made. First of all, it should be noted that types of RES are different in origin, as well as in their renewability cycle, therefore, classifying biofuel as a renewable energy source is a true misunderstanding. On the other hand, there is complete uncertainty about the impact of biofuel combustion on emissions. Climate change reports show that burning of biofuels generates significant CO_2 emissions, while, at the same time, biofuel is treated as CO_2-neutral in energetics, and is considered a "big achievement": in Lithuania, up to 60% of heat is produced using biofuels. This is the strangest and most controversial phenomenon in terms of combatting climate change. This extremely dangerous trend has already been highlighted by many scientists, specifying extreme pollution of biofuel combustion and the negative consequences of tree destruction as CO_2 absorbers. And yet the mass use of biofuels is called progress in terms of economic advancement, which in this case is in stark contrast to the logic of nature conservation. Recent European Union (EU) resolutions express a clear concern about such destruction.

Numerous facts show—and prove to those seeking harmony with nature—that a strictly anthropocentric and, at the same time, technocratic paradigm leads to catastrophes, and the only way to salvation might be the aspiration to change the direction of the progress that is particularly defined in energetics, in terms of environmentally friendly technologies. Technological progress in the use of RES is encouraging. This is especially true for solar technologies that are developing at an incredible pace and are gaining widespread application. In other words, technological progress and its evaluation require a new direction. The increasing use of RES, the application of circular economy principles, eco-cities and green settlements (communities) are new signs of a rebirth, the emergence of which is a symbol of a new reverse direction in nature, which could connect technological progress with the human mission in nature. The task of forming a paradigm of harmonious progress means combining the latest positive trends and theoretically developing these phenomena to reach, if not the end, then at least an intermediate long-term goal. It is necessary to lay down the guidelines for the transitional period, based on the latest technological advancements, the purposeful application of the circular economy and the mass ecological movements of people appalled by such apparent tech domination into art, science, and cultural life in general. The concept/paradigm of harmonious progress differs from the one-sided conceptualisation of technological progress and the pace of economic growth, in that it synthesises and summarises thoughts and knowledge that provide meaning to human existence and "reconcile" scientific and technological achievements with the eternal laws of nature's evolution that have been expressed by prominent authors long ago, even though they are pushed aside by historical thinking.

I strongly believe that it is essential to synthesise these concepts in order to make the consequences of the brutal destruction of nature evident through the education system and to shift the application of technological advancement solutions in the right direction—I call this "harmonious change".

Chapter Two

A Projection of the Paradigm of Harmonious Progression into Changes in Human Mentality

Changes in mentality in terms of the interaction between nature and man

Nowadays, harmonious progress can be described as what to modern man would look like an attempt to revive the thoughts, worldviews, and attitudes that emerge from the writings of the great thinkers of past centuries. However, to fully evaluate the essence of progress, it is essential to renew the bond between the philosophical origins of harmonious advancement theories, which are related to the development of evolutionary theory over the centuries, and the current worldview and attitudes that have changed in a very short period, and there is a significant gap. Some of the most significant and explicit scientific principles of ecological-economic organisation, which explain the dramatic change in worldview and mentality of people, were provided by Čiegis (2003). The question of the purpose of a human's life has long been disconnected from the laws of evolution, and even more so, humans' relationship with nature becomes consumerist, although the current situation of climate change shows that fostering this relationship is crucial. Evolutionary theory has undergone many changes due to critics and one-sidedness and currently has probably the least defined expression. Inevitably, the question arises as to the role of man in the context of the natural processes that take place, and ultimately in the realisation of man's goals and aspirations for life. That divide between man and nature, especially due to the incredible scale of urbanisation, should also find a place in the explanations of the progress paradigm. Technological advances seem to have interrupted the continuity of evolutional theory previously nurtured in the works of these great personalities: Goethe, Albert Schweizer, Henry David Thoreau, Ralph Waldo Emerson, Jean-Jacques Rousseau, Abraham Maslow, Erik From, Carl Gustav Jung, Victor Frankl, Max Weber, Vladas Jurgutis, Ortega y

Gasset, Vydūnas, Antanas Maceina, Friedrich Wilhelm Joseph Schelling, Hippolyte Taine, Lev Tolstoy, Mohandas Karamchand Gandhi, and many more. The common idea of all these thinkers, briefly defined, is the great respect for life, which is understood by recognising the laws that govern nature, including man, as a determining power of human existence. The great humanists developed a philosophy of the meaning of human life and human purpose, which viewed nature as the basis of humanity and even existence, and, in economic terms, demanded to look upon nature with infinite respect, and not simply as a source of inexhaustible wealth that could be recklessly exploited. On the contrary, human work, in harmony with nature, is a guarantee of health. The key question that links these global problems to the narrower theme of our analysis is whether evolution is spontaneous or whether a human is obliged to (or even can) guide human-Nature interactions in a positive direction.

History researchers note the inequalities of the change in the centres of progress, but against the backdrop of technological advances, there has been an over-reliance on the spontaneity of progress. Of course, the axis of evolution is unidirectional, but those incredibly rapid changes in human mentality that have occurred in a very short historical period are becoming a very serious threat on a global scale. Not only the coexistence of people but also economic phenomena can greatly depend on the assessment of the worldview. The modern period can be considered as a turning away from globalist tendencies towards what constitutes individual states and the people living within their territory. The scope of this enormous wealth of ideas is impossibly large, and it is not the purpose of this monograph to analyse and summarise it. It is simply worth mentioning that the synthesis of the thoughts of the previously named big minds can be considered a warning sign that, amazingly, has been completely ignored since Adam Smith's times, by the justification of profit-making ethics, or simply by forgetting his book, "Theory of Moral Feelings". From the time of Adam Smith to the present, man has been viewed as a *homo economicus*. Therefore, economic activity has become strictly determined and subordinated according to the motives of economic interests. However, as noted by H. D. Thoreau (1985):

> People's labour is marked by error. They plough the better part of themselves into the soil instead of fertilizer. The supposed fate, commonly called necessity, forces them to accumulate wealth. In fact, a person does not have the time to feel his/her personality every day, he/she does not even get in touch with other people—he would lose its value in the labour market. He has no time to be anything other than a machine.

As Bauman (1995) states:

> We are not thinking of progress in the context of improving one's status, but of avoiding failure. Often our only concern is to avoid failure. The struggle to prevent failure requires full, undivided attention, 24-hours a day, seven days a week. The consumer-oriented economy of fluid modernity is based on the abundance of its offerings and its rapid depreciation.

We can state that, for a very long historical period, humans have lived in ecological harmony with nature, at least to a greater extent (Norgaard, 1984). J. J. Rousseau called it a "golden period". This thinker came up with the slogan "Back to Nature" that should not be understood in a primitive way. His works represent a complex philosophical system that is rejected only because his theory is considered to be an attempt to turn history in the opposite direction. Our distinguished scholar, M. Gimbutiene, also wrote about the "golden age" of the matriarchate, as women played a vital role in the context of family and tribe. However, this harmony was determined by the small size of the population and the scarce technical ability to significantly damage nature, as well as the norms of social life that protected the natural essence of human existence. The concept of technological determinism was not changed by the Luddites. Even Luddites from all over the world could not change the current state simply by destroying technology or slowing down the development of technology. Technological progress adequately conformed to the provisions of the industrial era of human civilisation, which were born of the mentality of the industrial revolution. Currently, facing ecological catastrophes, we are forced to question conventionally perceived progress, therefore, new perspectives are emerging regarding the concept of progress. But it should be noted that knowing the consequences of negative environmental and human impacts (of which modern man is already well informed) is not yet a sufficient basis for a radical change in the way people live and their attitudes towards nature given the deep structures of individual and collective consciousness are not affected. The mentality in a country is not so easily changed, although after two world wars, the mentality of some countries, especially Germany, has changed significantly. However, some phenomena seem truly threatening. As Ortega y Gasset (1993) stated in his famous work, "The Rebellion of the Mass":

> The key feature of our time is the strange belief that it is above all former periods—it seems that it completely rejects the past, does not recognize the classical and normative epochs and considers itself the beginning of a new life that surpasses the former and depends on the latter. The sense of security

of the previous epochs, as the main characteristic of the 19th century, is an optical illusion. By believing in it, humans stop caring for the future—leaving it to the self-mechanism of the universe (Ortega y Gasset 1993).

Essentially, the laws of nature's evolution will last forever, but human evolution seems to be disrupted and distanced from nature, to which man himself belongs. According to Teilhard de Chardin, the modern concept of evolution is related to the process of evolution of the whole world, nature, and man. The great psychologist C. G. Jung (1999) said: "People are now a bit disturbed: they hear, read about the necessity of change, but do not want to believe it 'inside' because all of our daily experiences so far do not give the signal of deadly danger". C. G. Jung noted the phenomenon of this era, referring to the peculiar psychological phenomenon of the people used by the entire advertising industry.

> Freud himself, the pioneer of psychoanalysis, made every effort to bring to the light of day the dirt, darkness and evil of the deep foundations of the soul so that the world would never want to see waste and debris. But he failed to do so; on the contrary, these intimidations produced a completely unimaginable phenomenon of admiring the dirt (Jung 1999).

However, the alarms of danger come both directly and indirectly. Natural disasters and migration kind of demonstrate that increasing ecological disasters are just a "general rehearsal" before the further influx of refugees, flooding entire countries.

> There is a whirlwind of universal and all-encompassing farce across Europe. All forces are aimed in one direction—how to get away from your destiny. The average human does not seek to settle on the firm foundations of his destiny; it is better for him to keep living between heaven and earth. Therefore, today, there is an abundance of such weightless lives, rooted out of their destiny, that can be carried away by the slightest current. This is the era of currents and flyers. Almost nobody shows resistance to the whirlwinds of backyards, which have entered into art, philosophy, and social life (Ortega y Gasset, 1993).

The desire not for catastrophe, but simply for a better, more well-established life, compels people to leave their home country rather than create a better life in the destined homeland. And yet, the analysis of Carl Gustav Jung, the researcher of the human soul, shows that these needs emanate from the very depths of human existence. In Richard Lory's preface to Maslow's "Psychology of Being", he wrote:

> By the end of the nineteenth century, until about the mid-1960s, the general theory of human motivation had become so strong that it had become official party orthodoxy. Originating from Darwin's theory of evolution, the fundamental dogma of the orthodox doctrine was that innate motivation of the species can only consist of needs, powers, desires, impulses that help an individual survive or breed, in other words, selfishness, sexuality, and aggression. These are supposedly primary motives (as they are considered common to all or at least to the majority of people). Others are merely secondary or derivative; they are acquired later by the individual, as they appear to be useful in satisfying one or more primary motives (Maslow 2012).

But A. H. Maslow, being one of the pioneers of humanistic psychology, re-examined this theory and proved by research that higher human motives are just as inherent, and not derived. Thus, human self-actualisation or psychological wholeness can only be achieved through the realisation of these higher motives. In other words, the constitutional purpose of man in nature is not the struggle for existence, but the unfolding of his humanity which in no way implies the "defeat of nature". A. H. Maslow highlighted two fundamental principles of human motivation—motivation of lack and growth. He found an explanation as regards why the motivation for growth and self-actualisation, found in every human being, manifests in very few practical lives. "Most of us spend most of our lives enslaved in one or another level of lack of motivation. Higher and more human-exclusive opportunities remain locked, disguised, eclipsed, and cannot manifest themselves" (Maslow 2012). A. Schopenhauer, one of the most influential philosophers of the nineteenth century, known as the misanthropist, wrote in the early nineteenth century:

> The source of our dissatisfaction is the endless effort to increase necessities, although the other factor, resources, remains unaltered. It is not surprising, then, that in such a needs-driven and almost exclusively needs-based society as the tribe of human, wealth is the most sincerely worshipped; government is also used as a means of overpowering; can anyone be surprised that in sake of wealth everything is being forsaken in the world, and there is nothing to make the heart and the hand to shake (Schopenhauer 2001).

Modern economic theory is essentially based on a lack of motivation. That wouldn't be too bad, but this lack of motivation has degenerated into a desire for overconsumption, caused by mass advertising. Consumption, or the need for unnecessary items, has become an obsession and a flywheel for economic growth.

> Over the last two centuries, we have learned nothing but exponential growth and, in parallel, have created a culture of exponential growth that is so heavily dependent on exponential consumption for growth stability, that it is no longer capable of dealing with the problems of growth (Hubbert 1992).

The idea of a circular economy came up against this trend. However, for the circular economy to emerge, a lot of serious efforts that will be discussed below will have to be paid.

In essence, an apologist for the circular economy is H. D. Thoreau (1985), whose idea can be unquestionably endorsed: "Not only are most luxuries and so-called conveniences of life essential, but they are also a real obstacle to human progress". It's now widely recognised that over 15 years, from the late 1960s to the early 1980s, the Western world reached a mass consumption stage.

> Freedom of the consumer is becoming more and more freedom of choice, which is of course strongly correlated with the erosion of traditional cultural norms and social relationships. The ideological basis for such scale of consumerism is an undoubtedly neoclassical economic theory (McKendrick, Brewer and Plumb 1982).

Cities, especially metropolitan areas, are a particular junction of problems, but also a source of possible solutions.

The necessity and content of the transformation of economic theory

> The basic claims of the market economy were formulated at a time when the scale of human economic activity compared to that of ecosystems was relatively small; therefore, in economic theory and practice, it was possible to ignore the fundamental fact, that human actions are dependent on the ecosystems of our planet (Čiegis 2004).

Economic theory is based on, or at least should be based on, the fundamental regularities that determine the economic development of society. However, these regularities include the necessity of interaction between nature and man as the pinnacle of natural evolution. The challenge of the harmonious progress paradigm is to formulate tools that can smoothly address the challenges of a changing ecological situation. Economic theory combines individual economic facts into a coherent, logical structure of causes and effects, which allows the forecasting of economic trends and the selection of economic policy measures. Ecological conditions, changing in a threatening direction, and competitive struggle in the markets pose new challenges and force us to look for answers to which dominant economic theory has yet to respond. When the provisions (axioms, postulates) of economic theory cannot explain the difficulties of life and the struggles in the development of society, economic policy decisions and new hypotheses are raised, tested and recommended for improvement, new solutions are proposed, and corrections are made. Urbanisation has long since transgressed all the power of nature in an accumulation of pollution, in particular from industrial and transport flows. The rigorous and formal analysis of the neoclassical approach is the main reason why the dependence of economic production, consumption and welfare on natural resources and ecosystems is not assessed. Furthermore, the dependence on human aspirations and goals, which nevertheless exist as an imperative of evolution, is not assessed. As these theories emphasise the role of the market, natural resources were appreciated only to the extent that their value was reflected in the market, without (or at least not emphasising) the difference between renewable and non-renewable natural resources. Therefore, the cornerstone of the paradigm of harmonious progress is the emphasis on the economic valuation of renewable energies. I build my theoretical foundation on this premise.

After the international financial crisis in 1929, which was caused precisely because of the microeconomic point of view, J. M. Keynes (1964) formulated the principles regulated in the macroeconomic scope. Although the main microeconomic thinking regarding growth and development, ignoring nature, still exists. One of the initiators of the neoclassical synthesis, P. Samuelson, in his book "Economics", describes how market economics theory defines, at the macroeconomic level, how and why profit is the engine of economic and technological advancement when certain preconditions for the market mechanism are met (Samuelson 1983). However, this theory does not consider ecological threats, as it is simply not interested in them, leaving them to municipal legislation solutions. The dominant mentality is exposed in the following theoretical position:

> Even when private transactions cannot balance out private and social assumptions, it can be done by governmental policy. The critical question of policy is not if pollution exists, but if it is considered as being at the optimal level. The economic point of view as regards pollution control—keep the air and water clean with the help of mass consumption products, such as petrol or air conditioning, which must meet standard criteria, applied to all goods of such kind. The last unit of clean air and water should provide marginal social value, equal to the social marginal costs of its provision (Griffin and Steel 1986).

We should briefly look at the major problems that make it necessary to evaluate the classic postulates of neoclassical theory. Market economy theory, a neoclassical synthesis that prevailed until the 1970s, is a system of concepts that states that prices, in terms of social marginal costs and benefits, can be constructed through governmental policy. At the heart of the theoretical conception of this theory is "sustainable development", without limiting growth in consumption. But as the power of civilisation grew (disproportionately expanding), civilisation took over the entire planet, leaving it with no human-free space. There is nowhere to move. Humans have not evaluated the seriousness of this situation for a long time. However, this was one of the most important criteria, as a result of this neoclassical theory paradigm and propaganda, that gave birth to a special phenomenon—globalisation. The main problem is that all market mechanisms require that the only way for resources to be distributed effectively is for perfect competition conditions to be met, which is not even possible, as the phenomenon is simply an avoidance of competition. A microeconomic approach opens the way to uncontrollable phenomena. In the context of globalisation, national networks no longer have the capacity to make decisions to avoid a crisis. The global economic crisis in 2009 highlighted and turned the most important issues into problems that should only arise in ordinary conditions.

> The need to liberalize global trade anonymously has taken over the whole world without any public debate or questions as to the benefit. To some extent, the market economy is great. But when it leads to exponentially growing manufacturing and extreme growth of trading companies, it begins to threaten the environment and democracy. This is no longer a free market. It then moves from a democratically controlled market to a market controlled by the biggest market forces. Criteria for supporting the economic theory of free-market advantages are no longer valid (Norgaard 2001).

Thus, the debates that have been going on since the 1960s, affected by negative and ever-worsening ecological and social problems, have forced the situation to try to change in a positive direction and fix extremely serious errors in economic theory.

More evidently, this situation manifests itself in energetics, having the special meaning and status of energy as a commodity. Energy markets cannot ensure the important energy sustainability priorities themselves—security of energy supply, reduction of environmental impact and access to energy for poorer towns and villages, as well as wider use of RES, and the ability for future generations to have available energy sources. Research into these and other issues have highlighted serious problems which arise when evaluating various aspects of sustainable development in terms of economic theory. The problem-solving necessities determine the research directions, although a unified methodological basis is required. I will try to define the fundamental question of methodology formation in terms of economic theory.

The main methodological problem is that the cost analysis tool, as the main analysis method in economic theory, divides the market players into separate subjects of activity. Let me clarify this statement. An economic analysis, in terms of energy provision, considers the manufacturing of energy separately from the reliability of energy provision, environmental damage and social issues, highlighting the importance of ensuring energy provision for future generations. When economic theory is applied in practice, the main difficulty arises that atmospheric pollution and external costs are considered as commodities. I will quote the characteristic approach of the American school, defining the solution of the methodological problem.

> It's a widespread logical error, to identify the source of contamination, and automatically conclude that there is a market error, which is leading to welfare losses. It must be remembered that externalities exist when the private assessment of costs or benefits outweighed the social assessment of costs and benefits. Voluntary commitments between the polluting and the affected parties can help reach optimal results (Griffin and Steel 1986).

I have cited this relatively long extract that gives the point of view which is often seen as an axiom where certain deviations are possible but are considered to be solutions provided by economic policy. I would specifically exclude the saying: "Voluntary commitments between the polluting and the affected parties can help reach optimal results". According to this statement, energy reliability assurance and environmental projects are considered as an object of agreement among autonomous market players. But from the energetics perspective, this is blatant nonsense. An example of the consistent outcome of this approach is, for example, the international emissions trading system where the wealthy win, therefore, successful market players are the ones who cheaply purchase the opportunity and right to pollute nature. The microeconomic approach has its logic, but its application in practice leads to consequences that are opposed by the movement for sustainable development.

Even though the Sustainable Development Movement is striving to stop the negative effects caused by the growth of manufacturing and consumption, it admits the possibility of pollution but believes that there is a need to negotiate it.

Consistently, according to the prevailing economic theory, a method of explaining and assessing market errors arises that allows us to justify the correction of directions and assumptions regarding employing governmental policies (Schumpeter 1994). The negative externalities resulting from market errors mean that the private costs of individual market participants do not correspond to all costs, also known as social costs, and therefore economic policy measures need to internalise the costs incurred by the state or third parties through one method or another. For example, the cost of health care caused by environmental pollution is included in the cost in the form of taxes.

The challenges of sustainable energy development can, for the most part, simultaneously solve many important problems: competitiveness of energy markets, the reliability of energy supply, and environmental protection. The sufficiency of energy and other resources for future generations is the key issue for sustainable development. Addressing social issues and integrating RES into the country's energy and fuel mix are not less important areas of research, although, these are usually treated as parts of the single energy and economic policy. Specific measures are required to solve these issues, but they usually conflict with one another. One of the most important questions is the ability to ensure well-being for future generations without compromising the interests of today's society, as the reorganisation of economics in terms of a harmonious direction with nature is very costly, bearing in mind the harm caused to nature during the last few decades. Addressing competition in the energy market and, at the same time, ensuring the security of supply is particularly challenging.

Therefore, the task of the research methodology is to specify the problems posed by the requirements of sustainable development, to name them and adjust the method, not necessarily questioning it, but applying new data, allowing us to improve it in order to solve the goals of sustainable development more efficiently.

> Environmental paradigms, born as the response of economists to the debates of the 1960s, and based on the neoclassical model of a closed economic system, are based on legitimizing environmental damage, justifying it as an externality of the economy. This is the most moderate extension of marginal economic theory. Unfortunately, depletion of the resources and the legitimation of ecosystems as self-contained, inviolable values in the environmental paradigm are still not seen as a limiting factor for economic development and are still thought of in terms of the market economy. It is limited to damage control and monetary assessment, limiting the number of human activities harmful to the environment at the state and municipal levels, assessing the environmental damage (EIA) in the project approval

process, and creating relatively small protected areas (national parks and reserves) (Čiegis 1997).

However, countries seeking economic recovery are ignoring the effects of environmental damage for GDP growth. As V. Adamkus (2016) states:

> We have been going through a long and difficult period of a breakthrough in the last three decades—a period of retreating from nature, and radical materialization. There was virtually no movement of the Greens, as it was in its origins. Lithuania could not remain unaffected by this trend. During those decades, with the globalization of civilisation, with the pursuit of prosperity at all costs, so much damage was done to nature that humans began to respond and change.

From a resource management point of view, the key idea is to include all types of capital, understanding that the scope of human activity is so huge that it now affects nature, not less than nature affects humans, and these effects can feed into the quantitative and qualitative characteristics of human life. Proponents of the ecological economy, therefore, distinguish natural capital, human capital (and/or cultural capital) and manufactured capital (Folke et al. 1994) and try to evaluate resources and integrate them into accounting systems, productivity calculations, development policies, and investment planning. And yet, the neoclassical imperative of economic growth remains the most celebrated "sacred cow" and environmental requirements are seen as constraints on growth, therefore, there is still a stormy debate that is, unfortunately, dominated by growth and laissez-faire supporters. Approaches remain essentially anthropocentric and technocratic, though evidence suggests that damaged nature is beginning to hurt all *homo economicus*, together with the free-market apologists. The Brundtland Commission Report "Our Common Future" is also based on this anthropocentric approach (Mitsch and Jorgenson 1989). Even bearing this limitation in mind, progress in thinking must be acknowledged. The resource management paradigm seeks to economise ecology, and much of the effort is directed towards maximising the use of economic instruments. The concept of sustainable development, despite its limitations, has complemented the theory of the market economy with a widely used method of cost-income analysis (on the scale of enterprises as market participants) and social-welfare analysis (on the scale of the whole economy). According to economic theory, existing and emerging problems can be solved by balancing marginal social costs and marginal social benefits. The marginal social cost, besides the private costs of an individual company such as a power plant, must be assessed by the social cost, i.e. costs that exist but are not recognised in the balance sheet of the companies' activities. An example of this could be the incidence of illness and associated health costs due to the pollution caused by fuel burning for people living close to the power plant. People who suffer and lose their health actually lose what they are entitled to—a full life. Thus, external costs are still being borne by third parties who are not directly involved in the market transaction in terms of the deterioration of living conditions, and by public expenditure from social security funds for the treatment of illnesses, not to mention many other negative effects. It would be fair to methodically estimate these external costs and include them in the cost price (this is called cost internalisation) so that the compared options could be correctly economically measured. But as soon as you mention it, the screaming and gnashing of teeth begins, with free-market authorities playing the first violin. In my experience, I can say that the vast majority of economists in Lithuania do not understand the essence of Danish energy policy which deals with polluting forms of energy, which are essentially external costs. In essence, the prevailing view is that it is a volatile intervention in a market-regulated economy. From the point of view of deep ecology, which does not approve of the compromises in terms of damage to nature, new solutions must be sought.

One of the most important ways is to create demand based on the usefulness of commodities, such as renewables, moving from their present state to one that allows nature to be preserved. Social benefits include, in addition to direct benefits to the consumer, benefits to non-market participants, business entities or the community, who are not directly involved in market transactions or investment projects. An example is RES, which can eventually replace exhaustive energy sources, such as oil and gas. The social marginal utility of renewables, which is different from oil and gas in terms of ensuring the energy supply of future generations, is not systematically assessed. Meanwhile, securing self-sufficiency for future generations is one of the key concepts of sustainable energy development. Even worse is the fact that we treat RES as a single "mass" and, for example, solar energy is equated with energy from timber.

In the opinion of the author of this monograph, although each country has different initial conditions, i.e. technical infrastructure and necessary amounts of resources, the energy generated from RES should, however, be based on a long-term macroeconomic policy framework, the methodological assumptions of which I formulated in my previous monograph (Klevas 2015). This means, among other things, that a good and scientifically sound theoretical context is needed.

The territorial dimension allows us to fill a fundamental methodological gap which can be defined in terms of the development programmes of different territories. In my opinion, based on the statements of many authoritative authors, the usefulness to society of RES, energy saving and energy efficiency can be defined and evaluated only from a territorial point of view.

However, these phenomena require comprehensive, organically linked knowledge, which is the challenge of the new concept of the knowledge economy. In recent years, research on the knowledge economy has intensified, reinforcing the belief that the knowledge-based economy has strong prospects in all spheres of economics, including energy.

Chapter Three

Guidelines for the Harmonious Progress Paradigm in Energy

The vision of the harmonious progress of energy

Energetics is an extraordinary sector of the economy. Being vital to all forms of life, it has always been and is a flagship of true, and often, unfortunately, only alleged progress. Energetics is a particularly useful object for analysing the problematics of progress and its essence from the economic theory point of view. It can be stated without doubt, that billions of years of history of the Earth and nature, confirmed by palaeontological science, prove the existence of the laws governing progress. Discussions or doubts are raised only as to the substance and content of these laws. There is little doubt in the idea that the creation of nature with all its diversity was not the result of the play of random forces. Various factors have shaped the existence of life on Earth over billions of years. In terms of energetics, though especially for humans, for millions of years, there have been carbon, oil and natural gas deposits lying in the depths of the Earth—the main sources of so-called fossil fuels. However, over the last century, these resources have been used to such an extent that their GDP exhaustion was already predicted in the last century at the Club of Rome. True, discoveries are delaying the final exhaustion, but in terms of Earth and human history, a century is only a moment. The point is not just about that. The main problem is the measurement of economic progress almost exclusively by the growth of an indicator that has been criticised for a long time. At the moment, the race for economic growth is taking place without time to pause and essentially reflect on what that means. Promises made by almost all democratically elected governments, and sometimes their fulfilment in the social sphere, are based on the forecasts of GDP growth, budget revenues and their distribution. The solution to the problems caused by the scale of the economics and its much-desired growth always turns out to be unrealistic and unworkable in the short term, as most legislators have no addressee, are not specific, or have tasks defined only in the form of indicators. And usually, all is done without even thinking about the consequences.

The second most important postulate of the harmonic progress paradigm in energetics is that the process is left to its own devices and adjusted on all relevant aspects in the long run. Energy is a branch of economics whose functioning, while vital to economic development, raises major concerns in ensuring aspects that are difficult to quantify in theory and even more practically—reliability of energy supply, environmental protection, and quality of renewal. The theoretical and practical evaluation of these aspects is very important and is becoming more and more explicit when it comes to giving meaning to the sustainable development of energy and justifying its content.

However, the term "sustainable development of energy", which has come into being during this period, has a major disadvantage: it does not set limits on the use of natural resources and is perceived as a process of adjusting it proportionally to economic growth and consumer needs. Damage to Nature is seen as an inevitable disadvantage for the sake of economic growth. Even the international system for trading pollution emissions has been set up. It is the fetishism of growth that is the fundamental problem that emerges from the mentality and worldview of the current era that the present paradigm builds on.

Meanwhile, harmonious progress declares a deep ecology-based evolution, which means an evolutionary reverse process in which technological progress focuses energy development on RES, energy conservation as an alternative to energy use, and diffused energy, whereby smart consumers can also become energy suppliers. This requires a broad and well-structured knowledge of natural and social processes that lead to sustainable development and its evaluation. At the same time, harmonious progress requires some changes in economic valuation that are already named but are not precluded by recognition and practical modifications. For example, for many years, the critically acclaimed GDP indicator has stayed as a bastion, though it has not withstood criticism in terms of sustainable development. Indeed, many supplementary or modified indicators have already been developed, but it is the majority and their diversity that make it possible to counter-argue and disapprove of the failures of this indicator and do not allow for error correction. In many cases, it is based on fragmented knowledge which does not provide a uniform basis for the decisions. There is, of course, an infinite number of models designed to calculate the expediency of one or another development scenario, based on the principle of cost minimisation. However, not all costs are included in the optimisation calculations, which means that too often, renewable energy resources are considered uncompetitive. In many respects, public expenditure in this sector is associated with costs that are not usually assessed for the use of fossil fuels and for utility, which is not estimated using RES. The practical application of the concept of sustainable energy poses many challenges to the economic theory underpinning public policy and the problems of developing a sustainable development mentality.

Under the influence of the knowledge-based economy, a promising concept of the circular economy is being formed, the basic principle of which is the imitation of natural processes by the massive use of non-waste technologies and RES. The challenges of harmonious advancement in energy create the logical challenge of reinterpreting the role of the knowledge-based economy as a synthesiser of various dimensions, together with data from various scientific disciplines, integrating scientific and traditional knowledge to study the conditions for harmonious development as objectively as possible. The methodological approach to sustainable development itself requires far more knowledge of the natural and social processes that influence the assessment of sustainable development. The new knowledge has been used to develop green accounting, the ecological footprint and other environmental accounting models in the EU and worldwide. These models are increasingly being used alongside the basic economic accounting systems and tools.

Harmonious progress could be described as a utopian scenario, as the present-day majority mentality cannot accept the fundamental principles of deep ecology. From the point of view of deep ecology, natural capital cannot be replaced by man-made capital. In other words, nature is left to natural evolution, meaning that virtually eight billion people would be unable to take anything from nature that could disturb the ecological balance. Meanwhile, every year, huge amounts of rock containing minerals are taken from nature. Human activity has already become the biggest force changing the Earth. It is estimated that 57 billion tons of soil and rock a year are mined and relocated globally, and that is three times more than is transferred by all the world's rivers—22 billion tons. This is a guiding principle that may require centuries of lessons provided by nature and new generations of humanity.

At the moment, we can talk about a vision based on individual examples, new ideas and initiatives. Basically, what it means is that natural capital cannot be replaced, only supplemented.

Further development of economic theory is what constitutes the idea of the meaning of life: an attitude of respect for all living nature, expressed by the eternal laws of nature's evolution and a fair view of man's role as a performer of harmonious progress in life. Therefore, the long-term perspective, as the ultimate goal of harmonious progress, is a holistic view of nature based on deep ecology which encourages people to perceive their true identity as the meaning of the organic part of nature. It could even be argued that this paradigm is not directly related to ecology as a science. It is a philosophical ethical movement, fundamentally revisiting the functioning of the modern industrial society and promoting equality of all kinds, the primacy of natural law, and the preservation of nature as its greatest intrinsic value.

Main theses

1. The distinctiveness of energy in terms of economic theory leads to possible significant adjustments (energy conservation as a contradiction to increasing energy consumption, whereas in other areas of economics, consumption growth is an element of economic theory justified by practice); the ability to transform consumers into producing consumers; and the mass use of RES technologies.
2. Nature is irreplaceable. The quoted thesis is accepted as an axiom:

> The representatives of the School of Deep Ecology raise fundamental problems of human being, its values and social progress, and actively seek alternatives to man and Humanity. Therefore, deep ecological ethics is not so much about substance, but about processes, not so much about analysis, but about logical synthesis, a holistic view of the world, not holism, but reduction. It prefers intuitive sensual rather than Cartesian, experimental cognition of the world (Čiegis and Jasinskas 2005).

From the economic theory point of view, this is reflected in the concepts of weak and strong sustainability which describe modifications to the idea of sustainable development.

Weak sustainability (moderate ecology) is characterised by the fact that the total value of all types of capital must be constant, but, where necessary, one type of capital can be replaced by another. In this way, natural capital and natural resources can be used while compensatory mechanisms are in place.

Strong sustainability is based on the idea that non-renewable natural capital merely complements the produced capital and is not its substitute. Non-renewable resources can only be developed under natural market conditions, without exception and any compensation or promotion mechanism. The use of non-renewable resources should be significantly reduced and used only as long as there are no substitutes for renewable resources. The amount of waste and contaminants emitted should not exceed the capacity of the environment to absorb it. Sustainability ratios require all capital ratios to have units of measure.

3. The only basis that can form a coherent approach to energy development is an independent state that is responsible for its economy and the well-being of its people, one of the key features of which is a reliable energy supply. The notion that sustainable energy development is something separate to the pursuit of this goal negates the basis for consideration. The "National Energy Independence Strategy until 2050", prepared in 2017 and adopted in 2018, is finally ready.

4. The concept of the paradigm of the harmonious development of energetics already includes not only the solution of development problems but also the correction of errors or consequences to harmony with natural processes and the level of energy independence of a country. And this does not mean that sustainable development is something separate or can be started from a certain period. What's worse is that sustainable energy development is often seen as some kind of separate section in the overall scheme. The current technological structure of energy has developed historically. From the point of view of sustainable energy development, energetics should act as a benchmark of a self-sufficient, proportionate use of natural resources.

5. Harmonious progress of energy cannot be treated while disconnected from consumers. However, the concept of the user needs to be developed in order to understand the essential prerequisites for harmonious progress. Also, the reliability of energy supply is part of the complex phenomenon of energy security, which encompasses national, technical and many other aspects. In one case, for example, in terms of gas supply, we may consider large aggregate customers—the electricity grid—as consumers, while in another case, for example, a city or town, may be treated as a large energy consumer. A separate category is producing consumers (of solar energy), which is currently considered to be expensive, exotic energy resources, the use of which is supposedly limited. And yet, this is not a private matter, since energy is a vital sector of the economy.

To escape from the short-term, fragmentary assessment and look at the energy mix in the long term, we need to establish a common economic denominator for all aspects of energy use. This approach requires non-standard solutions.

The territorial dimension implies the implementation of the management principle for the assessment of sustainability aspects of energy resources—definition of the limits of liability.

6. Urban, regional energy programmes must be a viable form of organisational and financial integration of new technologies through the

Structural Funds. The integration of local RES can be significantly more successful if a reliable methodological evaluation of the positive impact on social, economic and rural development problems is carried out, i.e. in the context of regional development.

A fully-fledged economic policy is necessary as well as its most important legal-economic mechanisms, the application of which would make it possible to correct market failures and imbalances. The main problem is the mismatch between social prices and real prices. Based on the theoretical analysis, it is possible to determine the basis for the planned support of RES. It addresses the scientific and practical challenge of assessing the links between energy development and economic growth, as well as anticipating and justifying social and energy security challenges.

Of particular importance are the organisational forms of RES utilisation, which are gaining importance and recognition in foreign countries. These are various regional or urban programmes, where renewable energy projects address not only energy supply, but also environmental management (biogas power plants in livestock complexes or municipal waste incineration plants) in parallel with rural issues and many other functions in the context of sustainable development. Many examples are effective in practice: they serve the purpose of creating the market of RES together with their educational function. These examples need to be analysed, scientifically summarised and proposals adapted to Lithuanian conditions have to be made.

7. In conclusion, the centre of gravity of the economy should gradually be shifted towards solving the problems of comprehensive human education. In the current economic climate, there is a growing awareness that the supply of natural resources, material capital and standardised education is not sufficient to create and maintain a stable economy of high productivity and competitiveness.

8. The harmonious development of energy is primarily and foremost associated with the uptake of renewable energy. However, the uptake of RES is also a process of developing and disseminating technological, economic and managerial approaches, which must gain a unified basis by specifying to what extent and by what criteria RES are assessed and on what basis this solution is compared to other alternatives. In this area, the range of issues and opportunities for resolution is clearly linked to the evolution and development of the knowledge economy. The uptake of RES can be linked to the objectives of sustainable economic development: social (maintaining income and providing a living standard for the poorest) and sustainable development (linked not only to the economy but also to the environment). Due to its specific characteristics, energetics has a much

broader public interest dimension. It's enough to mention the problem of reliability of supply. Therefore, the question of assessing the social utility of the use of RES is of particular importance in ensuring mass demand.

The wider use of RES seems to be an attractive alternative, but it does not easily gain in practical application. The main problem is to ensure a stable mass demand for renewable energy. The main direction of the harmonious advancement of energy is the massive use of RES in parallel with saving energy in all spheres, including households, who will gradually become energy producing consumers. Certainly, this will be a long process with different implementation rates from country to country. There is a huge variety of different assumptions leading to uneven starting positions, but the special "Damocles sword" of the climate change threat calls for radical, rather urgent, yet thoughtful measures. A key role in this process can and must be played by municipal authorities which have a variety of levers and opportunities in terms of the district heating infrastructure. The problem is, however, that the individual knowledge of various organisations and individuals has not become a body of organisational knowledge of the city government. Although the Law on Heat Economy of the Republic of Lithuania (2003) imposes an obligation on municipalities to expand the use of RES in the heat sector, the use of this development has essentially become a mass replacement of gas boilers by boilers of biofuel. However, there are other alternative types of RES, which are very scarce and only rarely used, although the large-scale use of geothermal and solar energy for heating and hot water production is evident in foreign countries.

9. The scientific problem is the correct evaluation of the social utility of RES which may show the benefits that are not included in the investment decisions, e.g. the inexhaustibility of RES and, at the same time, the ability to secure the energy supply for future generations. On the other hand, treating all types of RES as a whole can be considered a tragic mistake. This is especially true for highly polluting fuel—biofuels, which are artificially/conditionally considered renewable and neutral. Some renewable energy technologies, e.g. the use of biogas in animal husbandry complexes, also solve environmental problems and can, therefore, be additionally financed from other sources. This requires a comprehensive, coordinated set of knowledge and its targeted delivery. The solution cannot be unequivocal because the problem itself is multi-faceted.

10. It should be noted that technological progress (in the light of global achievements) far outstrips the general level of education and, hence, the receptiveness to innovation and, in economic terms, the demand for new technologies, innovative forms of financing, and managerial organisation. For example, the sustainable development of the electricity sector is

inseparable from the idea of developing smart grids. It is an overhaul of the electricity system based on future technologies and innovation, the core idea of which is to develop closer cooperation between the consumer and the producer, giving consumers greater access to the electricity market. The development of smart grids would encourage the use of RES and promote the liberalisation of the electricity market. On this basis, the reformed electricity market system would promote efficiency in electricity consumption and production, reduce the environmental impact, promote job creation and, of course, reduce energy prices.

11. A new educational concept is required that focuses on the development of a mentality for the harmonious development of society. The concept of sustainable development imposes boundaries and absolute limitations on the influence of existing technologies as regards environmental resources and the need to absorb the effects of human activity.

PART II

THE RATIONALE FOR THE METHODOLOGY REGARDING THE HARMONIOUS ADVANCEMENT OF ENERGY BASED ON THE LINKS BETWEEN THE CONCEPTS OF SUSTAINABLE ENERGY DEVELOPMENT AND THE KNOWLEDGE ECONOMY

INTRODUCTORY REMARKS

The main driver of energy advancement is the implementation of the Climate Change Programme, using RES as the means for this purpose. This aspiration stems from the newly formulated paradigm, the cornerstone of which is the Law on Nature Conservation, which has, unfortunately, been forgotten by the majority of people. However, this is only the final destination of a long journey which requires a clear system with certain defined milestones. In other words, to implement such an approach to energy advancement, it is essential to further elaborate on the methodology of overcoming theoretical and practical challenges. The main goal is the preparation of the whole complex of prerequisites, including the system for shifting human mentality, and the professional training of specialists for the mass deployment of RES technologies. Experience has shown that uncertainty in public policies and uncoordinated efforts in different departments are the main threats to the implementation of successful change in this sector, therefore, it is essential to find out how to solve the underlying problems (Meadowcroft 2007).

One might think that the issue of shifting to a more sustainable point of view will resolve itself without a change in the underlying paradigm, in other words, without emphasising the imperative of conserving nature. However, bearing in mind that solid biomass (wood and wood waste) currently play a disproportionate role in the renewable energy resource sector, since almost all future heat production is expected to be based on biomass, it is certain that the old paradigm-based strategy will still lead to a roadblock. Biofuel is often misinterpreted as a renewable resource, even though it can only relatively be viewed in a CO_2-neutral way. The exact specifics and potential threats caused by the mass use of this type of fuel will be discussed later. In the meantime, it is sufficient to note that the great appreciation for the mass utilisation of biofuel is a clear path to destruction.

Therefore, it is necessary to solve the underlying theoretical problems that are caused by the market economy's inability to avoid the disastrous effects of fossil fuel combustion on the environment, by ensuring the reliability of energy supply and an adequate amount of energy resources for future generations. Extremely damaging stereotypes regarding allegedly contradictory support for renewable energy must be overcome by employing a thorough analysis of the environmental impact caused by different RES types. The uniform interpretation of all RES technologies, despite their differences in various aspects, especially as regards their regeneration properties and their environmental impact, is even worse. Capital-intensive reliability and assurance measures for energy provision would achieve a synergic effect if, in parallel, the commitments of the Climate Change Programme could be addressed. Therefore, it is possible—and necessary—to combine different sources of funding on a unified basis. Essentially, the deployment of RES technologies can solve many problems in cities and settlements, the localisation of which is extremely important from a territorial point of view.

The main goal is to base the methodology on harmonious environmental transformation centred on a unified energy advancement paradigm, by gathering all the necessary theoretical solutions, methods, practical tools and assumptions. It is, therefore, essential to mention an extremely important, almost fundamental, element of the harmonious progress paradigm. This is the rationale for the scientific method commensurate with the scale of the task. It is important to note that knowledge is an essential factor in the formation of the sustainable development doctrine.

The sustainable energy development movement emerged in the 1990s as a response to the urgent challenges related to climate change—the depletion of fossil fuels such as oil and natural gas—which have been forecast since the 1960s, and other issues, such as the price volatility of these resources.

The global rise in the consumption of energy and other resources raises a lot of questions about future capabilities to provide enough energy at the level of individual countries and humanity as a whole. The solution can be seen in the replacement of fossil fuels with RES. As a result, the issue of preserving Nature, which is mostly threatened by modern energy usage and transport systems, will be solved synchronously. However, the transition to the increasing use of RES technologies has to deal with the problem of the reliability of the energy supply, which is related to the huge capital requirement for the transformation of the energy infrastructure. The solution to these challenges can be found by employing a wealth of knowledge from a variety of scientific disciplines, although it becomes a serious problem when it comes to the specialisation of sciences. Therefore, to meet the challenges posed by the concept of sustainable development, it is necessary to find a unifying theoretical framework that would combine different aspects of sustainable development. The most compelling direction of the economic theory in this regard is the knowledge-based conceptualisation of economics which is widely characterised by its universality and influence in modern society.

CHAPTER ONE

THEORETICAL ORIGINS OF THE KNOWLEDGE ECONOMY CONCEPT

The influence of the knowledge economy

The importance of the knowledge-based economy theory is expressed by its significant impact in various aspects. Numerous studies have determined the main cause of climate change to be the emissions from fossil fuel combustion, especially CO_2. This demonstrates the importance of knowledge for proving the facts which are often controversial. The historic Paris Agreement was achieved due to the detailed, comprehensively presented and proven knowledge on the effects of fossil fuel combustion on the environment. Therefore, the accumulation of scientific knowledge about the impact of fossil fuel combustion emissions on the environment has allowed people to convince politicians about the necessary global rescue measures. Knowledge gained from the research and its synthesis has enabled us to highlight the sources of ecological threats: "Now we have enough data indicating that such critical environmental problems as a loss of biodiversity, land degradation, climate change, and biosphere pollution strongly correlate with the growth of knowledge" (Čiegis 2002). On the other hand, the main direction has emerged which may have a critical impact on escaping from climate change: it is the replacement of fossil fuels with RES.

> As a result of the increased awareness of the dangers posed by global climate change (mainly caused by growing global energy consumption needs), the need for the future of clean and sustainable energy is becoming of paramount importance. This can be largely realized via a large-scale integration of variable RES, such as wind and solar, which have relatively low-carbon footprints (Cruz et al. 2018).

In recent years, the consumption of fossil fuel and the mitigation of climate change have become major challenges for governments all over the world. To engage with these challenges, many countries are pursuing the research and development of RES technologies (Shen et al. 2010). In the past few years, the use of RES has rapidly increased throughout the entire world. These sources have been recognised as significant alternative energy sources for the implementation of energy diversification. Political support for RES has been growing continuously both at national and international levels. The industry of renewables could be important to generate employment and stimulate growth (Marques, Fuinhas and Pires-Manso 2010). Investment in RES may bring considerable profits; therefore, more and more enterprises will be involved in this field. The successful commercialisation of indigenous, non-fossil energy resources is expected to promote regional economic development and employment, enable the increase of national energy security and reduce a significant part of the increasing trade deficit for the import of fossil fuels. Of particular note is the role of RES in environmental protection (Panwar, Kaushik and Kothari 2011).

However, a new stimulus for the successful uptake of RES technologies is needed. The main aspect of this stimulus might be multidisciplinary knowledge of the positive impact of RES and dissemination of it to all interested government and population groups. In many countries and regions, renewable energy is already responsible for meeting a substantial share of energy demand. Progress in building new energy systems is already considerable.

The development of the knowledge-based economy has given undeniable impetus to the sustainable development movement, which was started and stimulated by the problems of energy development. In 1987, the WCED led by Norwegian Prime Minister, Gro Harlem Brundtland, united the environmental and economic development perspectives into the concept of sustainable development, which quickly gained international recognition as an advanced economic development strategy for the millennium. Its content highlights four main areas of energy development: a) the development of energy without affecting the balance of nature; b) the self-sufficiency of energy for future generations; c) the reliability and security of energy supply in a broad sense; and d) from a social point of view, it is the opportunity to provide energy for all segments of the population regardless of their place of residence (city, village). The development of RES covers all aspects of sustainable development: security of the energy supply, environmental protection, solutions to social issues, and energy self-sufficiency for future generations.

Economic research regarding RES has recently increased through the implementation of EU directives, with a particular emphasis on the role of the territorial aspect (cities, districts). The promotion of the widespread use of RES has been declared in the laws of both the EU and Lithuania. The adoption of the Directive 2009/28/EC "On the promotion of the use of energy from renewable sources" (EC 2009) required the development of a National Renewable Energy Action Plan for 2010-2020 and many other documents at a local level. This indicates that the development of RES takes an increasingly significant role in the energy policy of all Member States, including Lithuania.

However, the practical application of the conceptual statements of the knowledge-based economy has been significantly delayed. Many authors almost unanimously state that this lag could be reduced only if research and practical implementation can be linked to the progress of specific regions and cities. Therefore, one of the most important modern developments of the theoretical knowledge of the knowledge-based economy is the regional territorial context.

> This growing emphasis upon knowledge has been influential in shaping new conceptions of urban and regional development policies and strong claims have been made as to the potential of such developments for urban and regional regeneration, linking the knowledge-based competitive advantage of firms with that of territories defined at various spatial levels (Hudson 2011).

Consequently, the concept of promoting RES in terms of the knowledge-based economy practically means that the process of the use of RES technologies must be controlled and adjusted for all relevant aspects in the long term. The incentive system is determined by the entire chain of energy supply and consumption and depends on the specific benefit to be assessed, emphasising the right distribution of cost and income.

However, there are still problems which have to be analysed and evaluated; also rational solutions should be provided.

> In many power systems, the level of integration of such resources is dramatically increasing. However, their intermittent nature poses significant challenges in the predominantly conventional power systems that currently exist. Generally, the higher the integration level of intermittent power sources is, the higher the flexibility needs are in the system under consideration (Cruz et al. 2018).

This means that the development of the infrastructure in parallel with the use of RES technologies is of critical importance. Moreover, the infrastructure of district heating (DH) systems is very important for the heating sector in order to widely utilise different types of RES.

As the local government performs a number of functions in the energy sector, municipalities could play an important role in promoting assumptions for sustainable energy development. On the other hand, structures that could concentrate various financial resources, which are available at state level, are scarce in cities. These financial resources, together with private investments, would allow the development of renewable energy technologies on a significantly larger scale.

The meaningfulness of knowledge economy theory in relation to the paradigm of harmonious progress in energy

Of crucial importance is the choice of a scientific method that can be reliably invoked to substantiate the essence, assumptions, and credibility of harmonious energy progress. The previous section briefly describes the impact of economic theory on the emergence of global problems that compel economists, ecologists, sociologists, psychologists, and other professionals to pay more attention to the origins of these problems and to try to come up with new solutions. It is obvious that energy is a branch of the economy where problematic issues are most acute—economically and ecologically—in energy solutions. This is why sustainable energy development (I emphasise—not growth) is at the heart of any theory of harmonious progress, although, unfortunately, energetics is usually left out by economists. I must briefly explain this crucial part. On the one hand, energy takes many forms and is an intangible part of our lives. We do not seem to notice it unless there is a power failure. On the other hand, energy permeates the whole economy, all households, and limits the way people live in urban and rural areas. If it weren't for energy, people's lives would be less concentrated and centralised in cities and would definitely be healthier. At first glance, it would seem that the concept of energy as an industry is understandable and clear. However, simple surveys ranging from ordinary consumers to prominent energy experts show that the perception of energetics is too vague. When talking about energetics, large power plants, power grids and boiler plants are usually imagined, but the understanding of the concept of energy as a whole remains problematic.

Harmonious energy progress must be understood as an evolutionary process in order to achieve certain defined goals, but it remains necessary to adapt energy development in a proportionate way to economic development, consumer needs and natural resource utilisation. Proponents of deep ecology believe that the boundaries of the law of using nature exist. I absolutely agree with this idea. Therefore, it is energy that can be the flagship, i.e. production and consumption can be organically integrated into the natural cycle, by essentially transferring energy from fossil fuels to renewable sources. However, this goes hand in hand with the need to ensure the reliability of the energy supply. This is a far more complex issue for the use of renewable energy technologies than for the use of fossil fuels while addressing the related environmental and social issues of energy production and consumption. But technology is advancing at almost cosmic speeds when there is sufficient demand for it. As more and more solar power plants are being installed on the roofs of energy consumers, one more question arises: how can we ensure the efficient management of the generated electricity? Obviously, when the sun is shining, the need for energy is lower, so it is very important to store it effectively until you need it. Batteries and other energy storage devices are currently considered to be the most optimal solution to this problem. Modern smart grids can already handle fluctuations in the electrical circuit almost ideally and respond immediately to cities' energy needs. This requires a broad and properly structured knowledge of the natural and social processes that lead to sustainable development and its evaluation.

When defining the goal and tasks of the sustainable development of energy, it is necessary to understand the significance for the national economy. Therefore, one of the tasks is to determine the economic aspects of the use of different types of energy and the preconditions for sustainable energy development—the research object must be structured accordingly. Energy, as a part of the national economy, is to be treated as a branch that has a significant impact on all spheres of life, and a unified methodological basis is needed to assess this impact. In many respects, public expenditure in this sector relates to expenditure that is generally underestimated in the macroeconomic sphere and is nevertheless based on fragmented knowledge, which does not provide a uniform basis for the decision-making process. There is, of course, an infinite number of models designed to calculate the expediency of one or another development scenario, based on the principle of cost minimisation.

Therefore, it is my deep conviction to build on what has already been mentioned in the previous section—the influential and increasingly modern concept of the knowledge economy which emphasises the direction of economic development, in which knowledge creation and its effective use, instead of only capital, plays an important role in terms of value creation and promoting harmonious economic development. It is under the influence of the knowledge economy that the rational concept of the circular economy is being formed. It is consistent, at least theoretically, with the paradigm of deep ecology.

For example, the concept of sustainable development puts the issue of public interest at stake, which is ambiguous. The general view sees public interest as meeting the current needs without jeopardising future generations. From an anthropocentric point of view, future generations are just people. But human existence is inextricably linked to nature. Natural biodiversity is the foundation of human existence. The implementation of this concept raises a unique, emerging problem in the history of economic theory, which is to balance the diversity of knowledge in many ways and to find rational solutions to all aspects of nature conservation. This has led to the application of the principles of the concept of the knowledge economy in energetics, in order to achieve coherence in terms of sustainable energy development.

There are many definitions of the knowledge economy that highlight one aspect or another. The current growth potential in terms of knowledge creation, dissemination and exploitation is making knowledge an engine for economic progress, and its use is an important driver of economic growth. However, it cannot be stated that in the current world of growth, the knowledge-based economy is fundamentally different from the existing market economy. In essence, the old reason for lack of human effort—increasing competitiveness—is repeated. If knowledge and its management serve the same proclaimed competitiveness, as the highest value principle, it will still lead to the same impasse, in which the technocratic and anthropocentric worldview dominates. From a conceptual point of view, the use of knowledge must, to a large extent, be oriented to the competitiveness of goods and services and, thus, to economic growth. Thus, the investment must be directed not only to physical capital but also to the creation and purposeful use of knowledge. However, there are organisations—ministries, municipalities, subdivisions—which, under their constitutional responsibility, must seek the well-being of the people living in the area.

But the biggest problem is that economic growth is being pursued at all costs. Inconsistent development is achieved with lower costs and, at the same time, lower cost of manufactured products, providing a competitive advantage in the market. That is why even the concept of sustainable development (which I emphasise is still at an intermediate stage, where all ideology is based on growth) is struggling to emerge, especially in developing countries. Knowledge encourages consumers to choose products from the sustainable economy while ensuring the quality of their living environment for current and future generations.

The evolving concept of the knowledge economy has crystallised the structural elements of knowledge. Much of the knowledge is not derived from the individual efforts of our generation but from past generations.

Thus, knowledge is, by its very nature, a public good, the supply of which is not diminished when it is transmitted to another person. This attribute links the concept of the knowledge economy to the important feature of renewable energy sources—that these resources (e.g. sun, wind, earth, heat) are inexhaustible sources of energy.

This requires a broad and properly structured knowledge of the natural and social processes that lead to sustainable development and its evaluation. The importance of knowledge is and has always been relevant, but it is only in the last decade that the emergence of the knowledge economy as a distinct scientific paradigm leads to positive trends, at least in the sense that problems are more clearly articulated and proven.

The concept of a knowledge-based economy emphasises the direction of economic development, in which the creation of knowledge and its efficient use, not just capital, plays an important role in creating value and promoting harmonious economic growth (Organisation for Economic Cooperation and Development (OECD) 2000).

In conclusion, besides taxation and support, measures to stimulate the demand for RES are especially important in solving the problems of sustainable development. At the very least, a balance between supply and demand must be sought.

The evolution of a knowledge-based economic theory

We will be analysing the claim that the concept of knowledge-based economics and its development can provide a promising direction for economic theory. This could explain and direct the efforts of society towards the harmonious advancement of energy in the framework of solving the problem of the widest possible use of RES. The motive and explanation are relatively simple. The point is that both knowledge and renewable energy are linked by an extremely important common feature: the extent to which they are used. In economic terms, not only does the increase in demand not increase but vice versa—it reduces the price of final energy, which is an extremely important feature of securing future prospects in terms of resource scarcity.

In his book “The Third Wave”, American futurologist, A. Toffler (2001) distinguished three waves of civilisation that characterise the stages of energy use. After a very long primitive period—the first wave—approximately 10,000 years ago, the agrarian revolution gradually enveloped the entire globe. This civilisation was dominated by renewable sources of energy—human and animal muscle, solar, wind and water. The second “industrial” wave was based on industrialisation, which was a major factor in civilisation; the energy was derived from non-renewable sources, such as coal, gas and oil. And the third wave is a modern information revolution, which has been going from the mid-1960s onwards and has led to the development of a "super-industrial society", where technologies are based on quantum electronics, information theory, molecular biology and ecology. This society should be starting to increasingly use a variety of RES. The economic development of industrialised countries over the last few decades also confirms Marshall's (1961) statement that "the most powerful engine of production is knowledge", showing a clear shift away from manufacturing activities based on the processing of raw materials to knowledge-based activities and new technologies. The economies of developed countries are increasingly turning to information systems ("knowledge societies"), which are dependent on the science-intensive production of information goods and services (Hargreaves 2003). Without any doubt, there are also solid signs in Lithuania that the current industrial economy, where goods are essentially created by processing raw materials, is in a period of transition to the information and knowledge economy, where knowledge is the main source of value creation.

Sagoff formulated the idea that:

> While raw materials will be required constantly, knowledge will become an essential factor in the production of goods and services. The advancement of knowledge also increases the quality of materials and human capital. Gradually, the centre of gravity of the economy is shifting, or at least should be shifted, from the problems of producing new things to solving the problems of independent and fully-fledged man-making, as it is being increasingly understood that natural resources, material capital and physical labour are not enough for creating a highly productive economy. Human abilities are now the main "fuel" of development dynamics (Sagoff 1997).

Due to the extent to which knowledge is being disseminated, the economy is highly driven by knowledge which has become a key driver of economic growth. Information technology not only accelerates the dissemination of knowledge but also offers effective solutions to successfully running businesses. The impact of information technology and new knowledge circulating in the economy has become so impressive that increasingly, more scientists are talking about a rise of the "new economy" based on completely new rules and no longer requiring the old skillsets. However, the knowledge-based economy can only progress if its participants are constantly learning, if they take over, use, create and transfer knowledge that has already been created in the world.

Currently, there are many definitions of the knowledge-based economy, in short, the knowledge economy. Often, these definitions highlight one or another particular aspect of this science. The knowledge-based economy is an economy whose dynamics are driven not only by investment in physical capital but also by the creation and purposeful use of knowledge. Knowledge has always been important to the economy on a large scale, yet due to the vast growth in knowledge production, dissemination and use, it has become the true "engine of progress", making it a key driver of economic growth. However, the knowledge-based economy cannot be assumed to be significantly different from the current market economy. The role of knowledge in increasing competitiveness is constantly being emphasised. The complexity of its creation and transmission has been particularly highlighted by two crucial moments. First, it is an extremely effective and economically powerful alternative to the Western market model—it is similar to the Japanese market model that can successfully compete in the global market while still maintaining national identity and relative reservation.

> The economic success of Japan is particularly frightening for liberal Western societies, being the first non-Western, non-liberal society to overcome them. The Western economy is based on the belief in the benefits of the free market and individualism, whereas Japan is essentially about maintaining a closed cultural tradition (Gilpin 1998).

The example of Japan is very important in terms of the paradigm of harmonious progress. Without its natural resources, it has become the world's leading economy.

Another particularly important new phenomenon is the sustainable development movement resulting from the threatening climate change trends. Non-sustainable development is associated with numerous advantages in the international and domestic market, which makes sustainable development extremely reluctant and difficult to become the leading ideology.

However, knowledge can be treated in a variety of ways. As the primary factor of production, knowledge, as an organised cognitive process, is a relatively new research object in the history of economic thought. Since ancient times, science has been recognised as a distinctly separate sphere of human activity. Due to its importance in the development of new technologies between states and transnational corporations, it is currently gaining new appreciation, even recognition.

The essence of the knowledge economy is no longer only technological priorities, but the exploitation of knowledge itself. Thus, the knowledge economy is one in which the creation of knowledge and its effective use—management of knowledge, not capital—play a crucial role in creating value and stimulating economic growth.

At a global level, the dynamics of knowledge structure are well described by S. Strange (1998). According to her, knowledge is the fastest-changing structure of the four major economic structures in the world (security, production, financial and knowledge). Even though the final results of these changes remain unclear, the tendency can be viewed as a competition between states to become the leader in the knowledge structure.

Knowledge capital is the wealth of the whole society, which, being constantly created and nurtured, becomes an essential source of added value and, in terms of economic theory, the primary factor of production.

The key question remains, how are the types of capital used being compensated so that the sources of economic prosperity are not exhausted when consumed in the production process? Economic theories currently emphasise the importance of renewables and knowledge capital as the most manoeuvrable types of capital with no existing growth margins.

One of the pioneers of the knowledge-based economy, A. Marshall, stated that "while nature is subject to diminishing returns, man is subject to increasing returns, and that is precisely in terms of his wealth of knowledge. Knowledge is the most powerful engine of production" (Marshall 1961). This idea was later developed by J. Clark, whose analysis led to a rather revolutionary and influential notion that "knowledge is the only instrument of our production that is not subject to diminishing returns" (Clark 1973). This approach has been reaffirmed in a new theory of growth treating knowledge as the good of non-competitive property (Romer 1986). As the models of the traditional economy began to fall short of the expectations of society, production, and well-being, Paul Romer and his associates began to explore and create new models for long-term development. With the support of J. A. Schumpeter (1994), M. M. Solow (1974) and others, and considering the importance of knowledge for development processes, P. M. Romer (1986) proposed a new theory of growth. Since then, economic theories have recognised knowledge as the third most important factor in the processes of economic development (Romer 1990). The development and use of the latter promote the development of technology and its application to innovation. Thus, the solution to the problem of increasing the state's competitiveness should be connected with the increasing role of the knowledge economy in the country. Support should be given to the creation and dissemination of knowledge (training of workers, entrepreneurs, consumers) and not to other resources (work, capital or land of average-skilled workers), which are not key factors for competitiveness.

It is noteworthy that the role of technological innovation in ensuring long-term economic growth has been the subject of heated debate in recent years. New models of economic theory, called "endogenous" growth theory, have been formulated (Romer 1986); (Romer 1990). The essential feature of this model is that technical innovation—the development of new technological ideas or constructions—is endogenously driven by the choice of the private or public sector within the economic system, rather than exogenously as in previous conventional neoclassical growth models. Endogenous growth theory assumes that if private and public investment in knowledge is purposeful and targeted, and if it enriches workers with higher skills, the economy can achieve unlimited steady growth in output and consumption. The market, in response to the scarcity of natural resources, will automatically trigger technological changes that will lead to the protection and replacement of resources, and, thus, ultimately, to the mitigation of scarcity. It is true, however, that there is a prerequisite for stable economic policies and social institutions that will facilitate endogenous innovation.

Emphasising knowledge and ideas, the new endogenous growth theory, formulated from 1980-1990, argues that the emerging knowledge economy is an essential prerequisite for macroeconomic stability. As Meyers points out, the new endogenous growth theory explores productive functions that show increasing returns through expanding knowledge capital and, as a result, specialisation and investment in knowledge capital (Meyers 1993). K. E. Boulding (1991) considered "know-how" energy and materials to be the primary factors of production—not land, labour and capital. He, therefore, described the production as: "channelling energy based on a certain knowledge structure to select, transport and transform materials towards the product" (Boulding 1991). According to Boulding, economic development is first and foremost a process of increasing human knowledge, whose limiting factors are materials and energy. However, abstract theoretical positions take on significance only as they permeate into life. In essence, all new concepts are formed as the new knowledge accumulates—the market signals its response by prices.

The methodology for the harmonious advancement of energy is an organic element of advanced economic theory, namely being an apologist for technical progress, creating economic preconditions for preserving nature and ensuring the rights of future generations to have no less favourable energy, natural conditions and opportunities than the present generation.

As with natural resources, the assessment of the knowledge structure is highly uncertain. So far, according to the general thinking process, nature is a free source of value and an absorber of pollutants that are being constantly poured into it. However, the clearly defined consequences of its pollution or excessive waste have an extremely negative effect in that people pay with the cost of their health, whereas the state wastes enormous amounts of its budget.

The assessment of the knowledge structure is even more complex and, principally, it is currently only in the initial stages of reflection. As mentioned before, it is certain that there is a dual theoretical approach—exogenous (driven by external causes) and endogenous (caused by internal causes of structural evolution). In the first case, the country's progress can be linked to high-tech purchases, and in the other case, to pursuing the harmonious cultural development of the country.

The concept of the knowledge economy has strong links and interconnections with the concept of sustainable development. The concept of sustainable development arose when there was an obvious threat to nature caused by the enormous waste from the production process, which could no longer be denied. Clean air, which does not have a market price, is used by all of us for free—until now it has been largely free of environmental pollution as well. Nowadays, there is widespread talk about the structure of knowledge as a production factor that has an obvious value and even creates added value but has no market price, as it is essentially considered a public good. It currently means being educated by the public science and education system, although, in the open market, the price of science is still only indirectly measured, e.g., as brain drain losses (Shumpeter 1994).

The main theoretician of the knowledge economy concept is considered to be F. A. von Hayek. Individual knowledge accumulates in a spontaneous order—one that without the intended outcome of any conscious act, occurs naturally as individuals maximise their well-being. He considered the interpretation of the results of human activities, which had not been foreseen and planned, as a profound object of social science. These processes take place without the influence of conscious goals, and they self-organise to help fulfil individual interests.

F. A. von Hayek's theory is based on the understanding of knowledge and economic challenges. In his conception of knowledge, which is reflected in his work "Economics and Knowledge" published in 1937, and his publication "Knowledge in Society" in 1945, he based his thought process on the concept of "uncertain knowledge" and the idea of knowledge distribution.

According to F. A. von Hayek, individual knowledge is fragmentary. In his view, which is difficult to disagree with, the knowledge of the conditions we must consider is never concise or integral because it reaches us only as dispersed fragments of incomplete and often contradictory knowledge at the disposal of individuals. Knowledge is not a simple set of concrete ideas, but a tool to help people make sense in a changing world.

P. F. Drucker (2004) and A. Toffler (2001) noted in their research that the ongoing information revolution is changing all institutions of society, including business organisations. Cheaper information technologies enable more efficient internal and external networks. They have seen and highlighted the transformation of the traditional economy into a knowledge-based or innovative economy. The latter is based on the creation and utilisation of knowledge.

For my research, I chose a particularly important subject—the possibility of the widespread use of RES and the economic support for this concept which is undoubtedly the flagship of sustainable energy development.

In recent times, the increasing attention of scientists has been dedicated to the problems of the knowledge economy, supplementing this theory with important information and scientific literature in various regards. One of the newest and most important research areas of the knowledge-based economy is the transformation of individual knowledge and information flows (e.g. various pieces of legislation, amendments, etc.) into an organisational knowledge system at the disposal of certain employees, which would potentially allow an increase in the competitiveness of the organisation.

However, less attention is paid to and, in general, too little analysis has been done on the topic of how individual knowledge becomes a systematic knowledge of non-profit organisations. A particularly striking and relevant example can be found in the activity of municipalities, which perform the functions assigned by the state administration in a larger or smaller territorial unit—city, town, or rural area. Their ability to organise progress in various fields can have a very significant impact on a large scale. However, knowledge itself and various types of information flows are so rich and dispersed among individual departments of the municipality, that it is essential to systematise them in a methodology enabling the achievement of factual results. Previous research has developed the concept of the knowledge base for the use of RES and the structuring of the knowledge needed to achieve results (Klevienė 2011). The basic idea is that the structure of knowledge produces social added value only when it encompasses both the totality of knowledge and the educational system of knowledge uptake. Currently, a major scientific problem is emerging: the performance of non-profit organisations, such as municipalities, in the context of the knowledge economy. Knowledge, relating to sustainable energy development, especially bearing in mind the widespread use of RES, which are completely vital for the mitigation of global climate change, becomes not only the expression of the pursuit of competitiveness but more the implementation and dissemination of advanced experience, knowledge and know-how. In the current new-era economic situation, the main emphasis is placed on the dissemination of knowledge. On the other hand, it becomes an effective tool to achieve the principal goal of a massive uptake of RES technologies with a wide range of positive spin-offs—reduction of environmental pollution, stabilising the price of energy, especially heat, and solving a variety of social issues, etc.

As previously mentioned, a particular shift in the analysis of knowledge, as a factor of production and economic assessments, has been brought up by the Sustainable Development Movement, which was initiated and encouraged by energy development problems. The Sustainable Development Movement, which began two decades ago, is an attempt to tackle global pollution, financial crises, leaps in global markets due to the depletion of natural resources, especially oil and other energy sources, and other threats. The issue of sustainable development is enormous, but what is at the heart of it, is the preservation of natural resources for future generations. Economics, as a branch of science, is facing perhaps the greatest challenge in the history of economic thought: the sources of value creation must be justified in the face of huge global threats. There is a well-grounded statement, explaining that:

> Knowledge is becoming a strategic resource for business, and the country's information infrastructure as a prerequisite for business development is growing deeper and clearer. The use of knowledge means that relationships (social capital) and processes (structural capital) are very important and necessary for the transformation of knowledge into a product or service. It is related to the process of conversion—from the possession of knowledge (often referred to as human capital) to the use of knowledge—referred to as intellectual capital (Atkočiūnienė 2008).

Particular emphasis should be placed on the importance of transforming knowledge into what is needed for the well-being of society, which is not necessarily equated with an increase in consumption (Hargreaves and Goodson 2006). V. Barkauskas and K. Barkauskienė (2011) draw attention to the fact that participation in the knowledge economy is necessary because of the ability to constantly renew the economic and social system. All of this contributes to the intellectual capital development of any company or sector (Castells and Himanen 2002).

Creation of new knowledge and scientific research are extremely important elements in the development of the knowledge economy. In the dissemination of knowledge, two aspects are important—the development of knowledge dissemination channels (modern information technology, television, radio, press) and the organisation of knowledge supply (search, accumulation, systemisation and storage of knowledge).

> The conclusion is that rather than competition between education systems, schools and students, what is needed is networking, deeper cooperation and open sharing of ideas at all levels if the role of education in economic competitiveness is to be strengthened. The key features of education reform policies that are compatible with competitiveness are those that encourage flexibility in education systems, creativity in schools and risk-taking without fear on the part of individuals (Sahlberg 2006).

CHAPTER TWO

THE CONCEPT OF SUSTAINABLE ENERGY DEVELOPMENT

The genesis of the concept of sustainable development

First of all, I need to describe the concept of sustainable development, the basis for the paradigm of harmonious progress.

The first debate on sustainable development began in 1972 with the publication of the report "Limits to Growth" on the global situation of humanity at the initiative of the Club of Rome. The debate on the current situation and the future of mankind has continued for 47 years since this initiative. One may argue that the ideas and doubts expressed in this report about the sufficiency of resources—especially energy—for future generations may not be so acute at the moment, yet the problem of extreme pollution, which culminated in the Paris Agreement, following the recognition of the need for a radical change, is becoming increasingly topical and worrying. The principles of sustainable development were indeed expressed in one way or another in much earlier and broader ways than a simple economic perspective on the aspirations of human society, as expressed by R. Emerson, M. Weber, F. Braudel, and H. G. Wells.

At the United Nations Conference in Stockholm in 1972, global threats to the natural environment due to the booming industrial economy began to be addressed on a global scale. At the time, dealing with the growing problems of environmental pollution meant attempting to integrate legal environmental protection requirements, which limit economic development, dissociating it from social and societal changes. Many years ago, there was an attempt to highlight that natural resources are not limitless and that human activities in many developed countries are causing irreversible changes in the natural environment, which are dramatically affecting the lives of people.

The term "sustainable development" was first coined in the 1980s as part of the first World Conservation Strategy, however, it has since evolved in terms of stricter form and content. The origins of the concept of sustainable development included two major political approaches to the possible aspirations of human development that dominated the international debate in the 1970s and 1980s. These concerned a debate about the development of poor countries and the potential environmental risks caused by their low level of development as well as the unlimited economic growth of rich industrialised countries. In 1984, a special commission, the WCED was set up under the auspices of the United Nations, headed by the Norwegian Minister for the Environment at that time, Gro Harlem Brundtland. In 1987, this commission merged these two perspectives into the concept of sustainable development, which quickly gained international recognition as an advanced strategy for the development of the human economy for the millennium. In three years, the Commission produced a report named "Our Common Future", which was widely published in 1987 and soon translated into many languages. In this report, often referred to as the Brundtland Report, the concept of sustainable development was formulated: in a general sense, sustainable development is a development that meets the needs of today's society without compromising the ability of future generations to meet their own needs.

It is a multidimensional concept, where the ability to ensure energy supply for future generations plays an extremely important role. In Fig. 2-1., the essential characteristics of sustainable energy development are shown and the concept of sustainable development is more specifically expressed (Fig. 2-1).

The concept of sustainable development perceives the public interest as meeting the needs of the present society without compromising future generations. The definition of sustainable development, in addition to the traditionally perceived added value, also encompasses: (a) stability, (b) reliability, and, more generally, security, and (c) impact on the natural environment. Therefore, it is a very difficult and complex concept.

On the basis of the Brundtland Commission's Report "Our Common Future", during the United Nations Conference on Environment and Development in Rio de Janeiro (UNCED 1992), a fundamental 40-chapter, 500-page document was issued, described as the most comprehensive and ambitious attempt to define the action required to combine development with environmental interests. These documents must be seen as a political expression of the long-term work of many ambitious scientists and researchers, the result of a long and complex process of research and discussion.

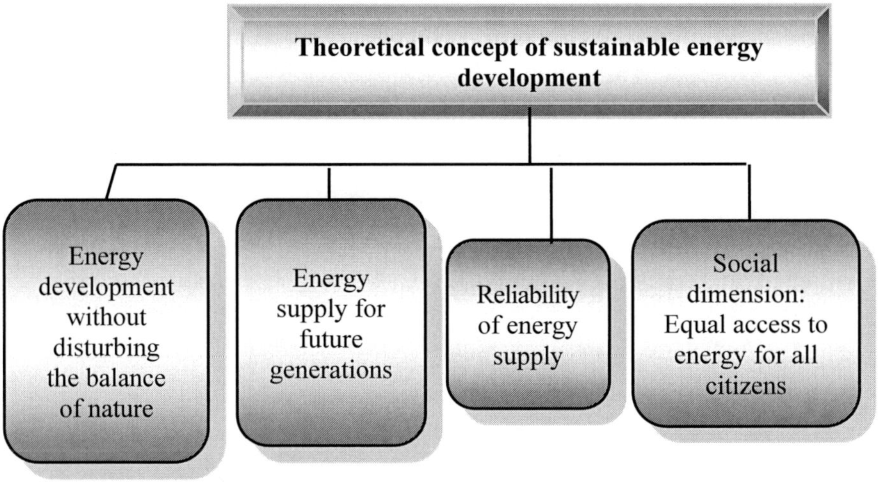

Fig. 2-1. The essence of the sustainable energy development concept
(According to the G. H. Brundtland Commission findings in the Essential attitude of the dominant paradigm in the interaction between nature and man)

The versatility of the concept of sustainable development has been clearly described by Pezzey (1992), who presented an excellent overview of the definitions of sustainable development and discussed in detail the physical, ecological, economic, psychological, sociological and, especially, historical elements of sustainable development. A similar interpretation was provided by E. B. Barbier (1987), who suggested that sustainable development should be considered as the interaction between three systems—ecological, economic, and social. In 2002, during the Johannesburg (Republic of South Africa) Conference on Environment and Development, scientists discussed the progress of sustainable development on a global scale. At that time, Lithuania also presented its sustainable development evaluation and strategy report (Lithuanian National Strategy for Sustainable Development), in which the achievements and shortcomings in the implementation of the Sustainable Development Criteria were presented in detail. One year later, on 11 September 2003, the Lithuanian Sustainable Development Strategy (Resolution No. 1160 of the Ministry of Environment of the Republic of Lithuania, 11 September 2003) was developed and approved, providing the list of 77 sustainable development indicators. In 2007, the list was updated with additional indicators—currently, it consists of more than 100 sustainable development indicators. Lithuania's Sustainable Development Strategy was adopted in accordance with the recommendations of the Council of Europe in Barcelona (2002) and the implementation plan recommendations of the World Summit of Heads of State and Government in Johannesburg (2002). The Strategy stated that the responsibility for the implementation and coordination of the National Strategy for Sustainable Development was assigned to the Ministry of the Environment. Other functions, such as constant improvement of the National Programme and participation in the biennial reporting process were assigned to other ministries (Ministry of Social Security and Labour, Ministry of Transport, Ministry of Health, Ministry of Economy, Ministry of Foreign Affairs, Ministry of the Interior, and Ministry of Agriculture).

Sustainable development covers all economic, social and environmental activities and is a comprehensive tool for assessing the impact of economic activity. The legal acts and resolutions adopted in the energy sector since 2002, in one way or another, are related to the implementation of the sustainable development criteria. The National Energy Strategy (approved by the Government of the Republic of Lithuania on 18 January 2007, No. X-1046) defined that strategic energy objectives will be implemented in accordance with the criteria of sustainable energy development. The Law on Energy, the Law on Electricity and the Law on the Heat Sector stipulate that the activities of the energy sector shall be carried out without harming the environment and taking into account the objectives of sustainable energy development. The purpose of the Renewable Energy Act (issued on 12 May 2011, No. XI-1375) is to ensure sustainable development through the use of RES. The European Union Directive 2012/27 / EU on energy efficiency and Directive 2009/28 / EC on motivating the use of energy from renewable sources as well as other energy sector directives focus on sustainable development and implementation. Sustainable development and its criteria have been widely studied and analysed in official documents of the European Commission (EU, EC). A great deal of information on the Sustainable Development Criteria and their implementation can be found on the official websites of the European Energy Agency (EEA) and the World Energy Agency (IEA). Sustainable development and related documents are presented in reports and documents of various international organisations. Many official documents can be found on the website of European Statistics (Eurostat), the Food and Agriculture Organisation of the United Nations (FAO), the International Atomic Energy Agency (IAEA), as well as on the website of the OECD. Reports produced by the United Nations Development Programme (UNDP) and the World Health Organization (WHO) provide a comprehensive overview of achievements in sustainable development.

However, the ecological status of the global climate situation is steadily deteriorating. This has influenced the signing of an incredibly significant global document in 2015, on the coordination of important measures aimed at combatting climate change.

> 2015 was a year of commitments. First in New York world leaders adopted new Sustainable Development Goals to rid the world of poverty, improve health, protect our environment and work through partnerships. Later in Paris countries agreed on the historic Paris climate agreement inspiring emission reduction commitments from virtually all nations. These efforts are intrinsically linked. From now on every year has to be a year of action. To achieve the goals set in the Paris agreement—to limit global warming to well below 2°C and pursue efforts to keep it at only 1.5°C—countries need to ramp up their climate efforts significantly. And we need to do it fast. Like the global Green to Scale report released last year, the Nordic study shows that there are already plenty of proven low-carbon solutions available, and at an affordable cost. There is no reason to wait. The time to deliver is now. (Nordic Council of Ministers 2019).

In Lithuania, strategic thinking in the energy sector has created an unprecedented version of the energy strategy, which defined the main goal of securing the energy supply almost exclusively on the basis of RES technologies by 2050. However, the most important problem in terms of sustainable development has remained: in the heat sector, the use of biofuels is defined as the main source of renewable energy. However, biofuel can only be partly treated as renewable, as it is produced on the basis of local forestry activities. In addition, combustion of biofuel is one of the most polluting and CO_2-emitting technologies. Strangely enough, this controversial fact is either denied or considered irrelevant, since uncut trees can eventually lead to increased CO_2 emissions.

CHAPTER THREE

CHARACTERISTICS OF THE LINKS BETWEEN SUSTAINABLE DEVELOPMENT AND KNOWLEDGE ECONOMY CONCEPTS

The key problem as regards the harmonious development of energy is that climate change emissions are largely generated by the process of transforming (burning) fossil fuels, especially in the transport sector. Therefore, the most rational and obvious direction for energy transformation should be the mass utilisation of RES technologies. This ambition is declared to be strategic in many countries, including Lithuania, but its implementation process is essentially treated as market-driven, based on a short-term microeconomic cost-benefit assessment. The implementation is, therefore, staggered, fragmented and uncoordinated as a whole. The aforementioned economic assessment and the levelled approach of RES, despite their differences in various aspects—specifically, in their environmental impact and the nature of their regeneration—have led to a huge disproportion in their uses so that investments are made mainly in biofuels, the combustion of which causes a highly polluting effect on the environment. Therefore, there is a need for an economic evaluation of the advantages provided by the use of RES technologies in terms of regeneration/recovery, ensuring sustainable energy provision for future generations, and not only comparing it with fossil fuels but also against each type of technology. Other types of RES, e.g., the use of solar energy, blurs the boundary between energy producers and consumers, as the number of energy-generating consumers becomes infinite; on the other hand, it is leading to major changes in the reliability of the energy supply. It is more than clear that it is essential to develop smart grids that could reinforce and transform the existing heat and power provision infrastructure and the methodological concept of urban energy. In order to give a sense to the new type of energy development, it is essential to create a system that defines the goals and methods for the professional training of industry specialists and the formation of the new mentality of people.

Although the research on RES is quite intensive, it is mainly concentrated on the application of individual RES technologies. In the social sciences, the main research directions are related to the RES economic support policy: a) various financial risks and analyses, measures to overcome the problems, stopping the development of RES sectors; (b) estimating the external costs of conventional energy sources, oil and petroleum products, natural gas and coal combustion; (c) use of RES-related technologies, economic analysis and evaluation of their positive impact. The amount of research dedicated to the development of RES at an urban energy system level is relatively small. The projects initiated by the Lithuanian Energy Institute, in cooperation with cities' administrations, regarding the organisation of RES in various aspects, are also worth mentioning.

It may be stated that this methodological approach is emerging as relatively new, although, many years of research have inspired the need for this methodological concept. In fact, studies have already been conducted and exact data revealed, covering possibly every single research direction of RES in foreign literature. However, the issue of treating energy progress as a holistic methodology, as a tool for climate change mitigation, has not yet been addressed. A number of policics initiated at EU level in regard to urban energy, which are subject to intensive research, design and initiatives, might be considered as partly fulfilling this goal. For example, the EU's Urban Agenda promotes improved law-making, easier access to financial tools and knowledge-building on important questions for cities. The EU Covenant of Mayors brings together thousands of municipalities, voluntarily committed to meeting EU climate and energy goals in cities.

Solving theoretical and practical challenges on the basis of a revolutionary idea of progress in energy development determines a coherent methodology for its implementation, including analyses of the challenges faced by market economies, justifying solutions by rating RES technologies depending on their environmental impact, and meeting the climate change commitments by employing city programmes and individual projects. The main governmental support measure should be the construction of infrastructure to ensure a reliable energy supply.

The most important practical value of this methodology is that it combines the two major programmes of this age—the Energy Strategy and the Climate Change Programme—into a single methodological framework. The methodology of energy development, besides the energy effect, simultaneously ensures the implementation of the defined climate change commitments—the synergies are achieved in terms of investments.

The energy transformation from fossil fuels, currently causing extreme exhaustion and pollution, to RES is generally considered as an expression of the progress of life, as it reduces environmental pollution, avoids the risk of morbidity, and reinvigorates the environment-friendly mindset.

In many ways, the problem is that the concepts do not match the content. Before defining the theoretical concept of the harmonious progress of energy, it is necessary to define energy as a whole. Strangely, it is one of the most difficult concepts to define. The main reason for viewing energy sources as a whole is that it allows us to compare all possible, existing and potential current and future energy sources, as well as to improve energy conservation and energy efficiency, comparing alternative energy sources.

What to choose: sum or totality of energy sectors? But then the issue is divided into separate, seemingly unrelated sectors. Then the need arises to distinguish between "indigenous" energy, which is still very scarcely noted. There is little data on this issue and, so far, it has not been properly addressed.

Fig. 2-2 shows the interaction between the concepts of the knowledge-based economy and sustainable energy development. It identifies some of the interaction elements which are considered in the context of measuring theoretical and practical problems. The concept of sustainable energy development is extremely progressive, corresponding to the respect for life in all its manifestations. The potential impact of the knowledge economy can play a key role in shaping the direction and coherence of energy sustainability. The broader societal scope of energy and further development potential make it easier to target the necessary research and choose the right economic policy instruments.

Fig. 2-2 (next page). Schematic of the formation of methodology for the harmonious progress of energy

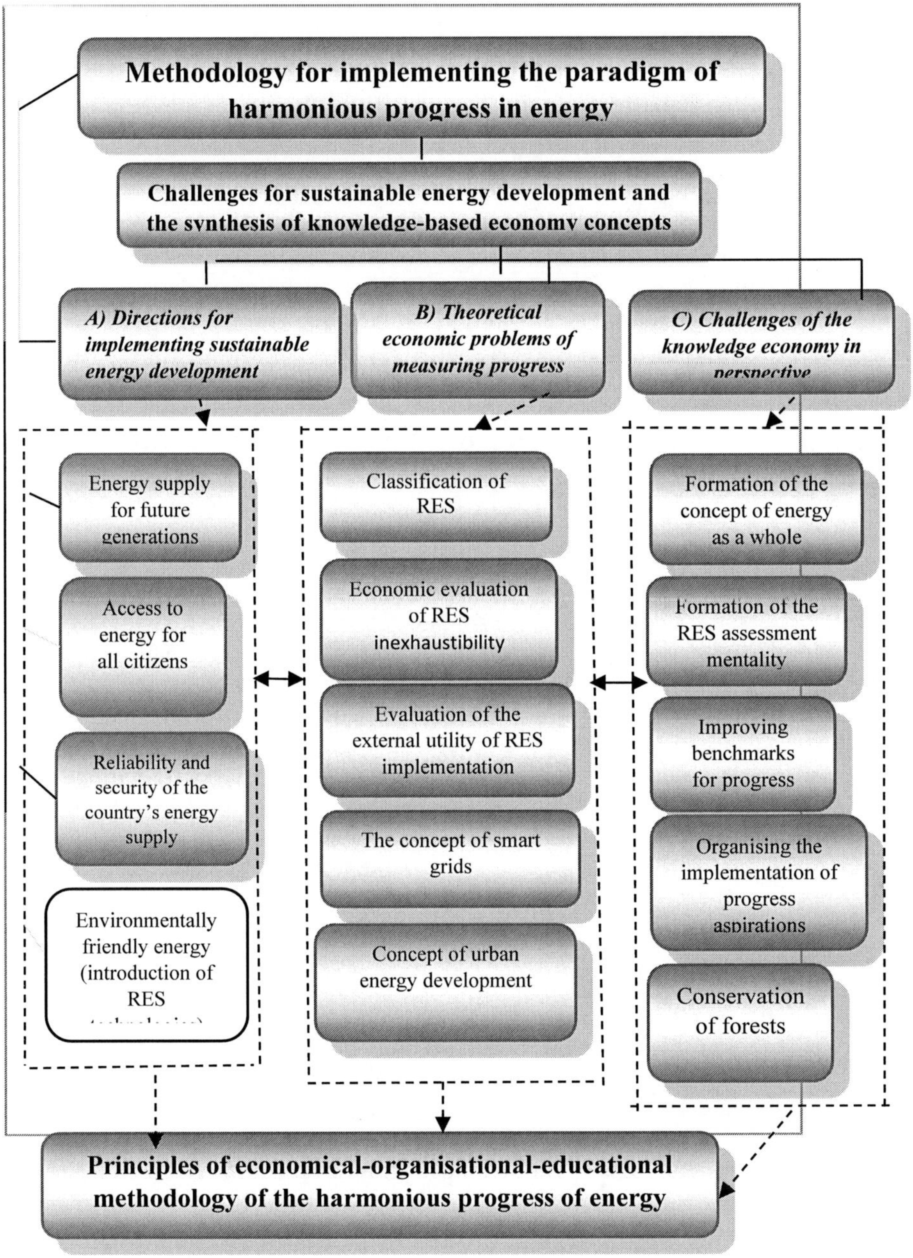
Methodology for implementing the paradigm of harmonious progress in energy
Challenges for sustainable energy development and the synthesis of knowledge-based economy concepts
A) Directions for implementing sustainable energy development
B) Theoretical economic problems of measuring progress
C) Challenges of the knowledge economy in perspective
Energy supply for future generations
Access to energy for all citizens
Reliability and security of the country's energy supply
Environmentally friendly energy (introduction of RES
Classification of RES
Economic evaluation of RES inexhaustibility
Evaluation of the external utility of RES implementation
The concept of smart grids
Concept of urban energy development
Formation of the concept of energy as a whole
Formation of the RES assessment mentality
Improving benchmarks for progress
Organising the implementation of progress aspirations
Conservation of forests
Principles of economical-organisational-educational methodology of the harmonious progress of energy

Let me briefly comment on the essence of the concept. In the diagram, the essence of the concept is highlighted by characterising the three blocks:

A) Directions for implementing sustainable energy development. Although already mentioned, in 1987, the WCED, led by Norwegian Prime Minister, Gro Harlem Brundtland, combined environmental and economic development perspectives into the concept of sustainable development, which quickly gained international recognition as an advanced strategy for the development of the human economy for the millennium. Even though the definition of sustainable development is not unambiguous and is actually a compromise, in terms of energy, its content emphasises four main directions which, if followed, can help to address the required issues. These are: (a) the evolution of energy without disturbing the balance of nature; (b) the supply of energy to future generations; (c) the reliability of the energy supply and, more generally, security; (d) from a social point of view, access to energy for all sectors of the population, regardless of where they live (urban vs rural areas). Almost 30 years have passed since the mentioned event, and a lot of serious problems have emerged, one of which is the compatibility of the stated aspirations, their harmonisation, and the setting of value-based priorities.

The issue of energy supply for future generations plays a key role in the multidisciplinary concept of sustainable energy development. The analysis of contemporary concepts of economic development highlights the crucial role of knowledge-based economic theory. It is noteworthy that both knowledge and renewable energy are linked by an extremely important connection: securing a future perspective in terms of resource scarcity. It is widely accepted by economists that the ability of a person to improve his or her knowledge is a resource that does not expire and can also exponentially grow over time. This is how it is linked to renewable energy sources—when the demand grows, the technology becomes cheaper. The structure of knowledge acquires the status of a primary factor of production. The challenges of sustainable development in the energy sector lead to the logical task of integrating scientific and traditional knowledge in order to study the conditions for truly sustainable development. However, the key challenge of the knowledge economy is to structure knowledge by developing a unified methodology for sustainable development. More than commodities or credits created by a financial structure, knowledge is inherently a public good. The fact that another person has knowledge does not diminish the supply of this exact knowledge to anyone else. This attribute links the concept of the knowledge economy to a very important feature of RES, namely, RES (sun, wind, earth heat) being an inexhaustible source of energy. This basic knowledge creates the basis for the commonality of society on the key issues of progress.

The practical and theoretical problems of implementing these directions raise both scientific and practical discussions which are far from being exhausted. The Brundtland Commission report "Our Common Future", started in 1987, has not expired; over time, it has acquired tendencies towards practical implementation. Although the inertia of energy as a branch of the economy is very strong and progresses rather slowly, some truly active steps are being taken. Even though at the end of 2015 the world leaders signed the Paris Agreement to Halt Climate Change—which demonstrates the global importance of this problem—this is only the beginning of a major change in energy policy for most countries. Never before has there been such a unanimous decision on any other issue. It proves that there is a widespread perception that the main source of climate change is the burning of fossil fuels and their products in the energy and transport sectors. However, there are additional factors, such as deforestation in many parts of the world. The main focus is placed on deforestation in the Amazon, but, paradoxically, so-called biofuels, and large-scale deforestation in Europe and Lithuania, under the same pretext of stopping climate change, is one of the strangest phenomena in human history. Therefore, in order to stop climate change, it is necessary to match the visions of often conflicting goals of sustainable development, which is an extremely difficult and complex task. Due to the specifics of energy, economic theory cannot prescribe particular means to link the pursuit of various, sometimes very contradictory, goals. For example, the promotion of RES technologies supposedly contradicts the market economy. However, this is an individual, purely theoretical approach, based on the claims of Smith's theory, stated two hundred years ago. If economic theory statements (axioms, postulates) cannot explain the difficulties of life and societal development by recommending economic policy decisions, it is necessary to raise new hypotheses, test them and recommend necessary improvements, solutions and corrections. This monograph suggests how synthesising the theoretical concepts of sustainable development and the knowledge economy can help achieve this goal.

B) Challenges of economic theory in solving sustainable development issues

The specifics of energy make it impossible to solve problems within the usual framework of economic theory, and even more so at a microeconomic level. Sustainable energy development is a long evolutionary process towards synchronised and coordinated implementation in all directions. The compatibility of these different aspirations in terms of the knowledge economy has to be addressed by subordinating all directions to the short-term and long-term reliability and security of the energy supply.

However, certain preconditions are necessary in order to achieve this goal, the most important of which are: a) various fuels and energies, currently valued as uncompetitive, can find potential applications only in the long term; (b) the concept of the reliability of the energy supply is much broader than is commonly understood. In a knowledge-based economy, this also means ensuring energy provision for future generations, increasingly incorporating RES; and (c) the concept of the reliability of the energy supply must be accompanied by price stability. Energy price stability can be most realistically achieved using a mixture of fuels rather than switching between different types of fuels, as has been done in the DH system for the last two decades.

Developing the concepts of external costs and external utility is a particularly important task. The importance of these economic phenomena has been highlighted while implementing the goals of sustainable development. These concepts and their content are theoretically grounded but do not spread to the public as a clearly understandable truth. Without assessing these economic phenomena, even the most professional economists do not associate fossil fuel taxation policies with the external costs of burning fossil fuels. This is because the enormous environmental damage, commonly referred to as external costs caused by the combustion of conventional fuels—coal, petroleum products, natural gas—is not reflected in the price. As a result, due to unequal competitive conditions, financial support measures are required.

The main problem to be addressed is making sure RES are treated as a unified system. In other words, the levelled influence (usefulness) of RES utilisation leaves a lot of room for uncertainty and subjective interpretations. This has implications for the large-scale uptake of RES and energy-saving technologies on GDP, foreign trade balances, and creating the economic preconditions for justifying government support. What is more, different types of RES vary significantly in various aspects. The classification of RES, according to the nature of renewability, is very important for the assessment of the expectations of their use in the future and for the implementation of corresponding economic measures. Therefore, using a classification based on the nature of the resource's regeneration, which defines the key differences between different types of RES, is recommended.

It is essential to find a solution to the conflict between sustainable development, focused on a very distant perspective, and the maximisation of welfare. The main idea is to ensure equal wealth distribution between different generations. RES already has an important role to play, especially considering the future perspective. The concept of sustainable development states that adequate support for RES is necessary because the market mechanism cannot provide sufficient impetus for the penetration of RES into the market. This support must be based on the external utility to society, which depends on the type of RES.

Another important issue is the evaluation of credibility and progress of other sustainable development directions in the territorial aspect. The territorial aspect allows the implementation of a management principle, evaluating the directions of resource sustainability and, at the same time, defining the responsibilities. The territorial aspect allows us to fill the huge methodological gap, which basically arises from the unsolved challenge of end-user demand, which is being influenced by the usefulness of goods and services. From the economic theory point of view, the usefulness of RES, energy saving and energy efficiency to society can be defined and evaluated only from a territorial point of view.

C) The third block identifies critical systems of knowledge creation, structuring, management and dissemination. Even the most rational scientific insights cannot help to make informed decisions, due to the resistance that comes from the microeconomic understanding of problems. Our analysis shows that most problems are explained more clearly and smoothly within the framework of the knowledge economy. Knowledge from a variety of sources, properly subordinated and proven, can provide the right solutions for economic energy policy. More importantly, the market does not capture the positive impact on the environment and social welfare that the extensive use of RES can offer. Therefore, a proper presentation of knowledge is an extremely important task.

Concepts that focus on the microeconomic market perception and the criteria of cheapness, which undermines important energy achievements in solving energy security and reliability issues, are featured in today's popular circulation of the energy debate.

From a knowledge economy point of view, it is necessary to choose an energy research base that covers the whole, as we are talking about different aspects that can be difficult to assess economically. Therefore, we follow actual, time-tested methodological tools that allow us to express the whole energy policy of the country: 1) Energetics is an industry whose "commodity" is energy, which can be subdivided into physical units, e.g. joules, kilowatt-hours, tonnes of oil equivalent, and so on. (2) For a detailed analysis of energy consumption, fuel and energy balance shall be used. It is a practical, internationally approved and legally valid statistical method of energy evaluation in the country. It provides a wealth of information on Lithuania's energy situation and allows us to compare it with other countries' energy development estimates. (3) When selecting the entirety of all energy and fuel types for the study base, it may be grouped as follows: (a) national; (b) cities, settlements; (c) energy suppliers; and (d) energy consumers who can produce their own energy and transfer it to the grid. With the widespread adoption of smart technologies in electricity and heat grid systems, manufacturers and consumers will not only be able to exchange data remotely but will also be able to exchange and transfer energy via two-way communication. That is, consumers will be able to become energy producers, and existing producers will be able to transfer energy where it is needed; smart technologies will automatically control these energy flows. One important element in this user-producer chain is energy storage technology and automatic power distribution stations, which must guarantee the security and reliability of the supply. In order to evaluate the environmental, social and renewable aspects of the use of energy resources, structured territorial use analysis of energy resources is necessary, since not all energy resources can be assessed equally in terms of energy security, environmental or social effects. Any anonymous assessment that does not have a specific territorial addressee may be meaningless unless it is based on the specific needs and problem solutions of the city or of any territorial unit. Therefore, there is a clear need for organised activities at city, territorial and government levels. Cost-income calculations must be based on the selection of organisational, management, and economic measures at various levels: state, regional, district, city, individual power producers, suppliers, and consumers. The main challenge is to synthesise various aspects of evaluation in a single programme.

Methodological approaches to sustainable energy development require much more knowledge of the natural processes resulting from the assessment of sustainable development. Moreover, solutions to the problems of sustainable energy development require the synthesis of knowledge and data produced by various scientific disciplines. The knowledge that was employed to evaluate the negative facts was also used to develop environmental accounting, green accounting, the ecological footprint, and other environmental accounting models in the EU and worldwide. As a result, they are increasingly being used alongside basic economic accounting systems and tools. The concept of a knowledge-based economy identifies society's receptiveness and motivation for innovation as one of its main objectives.

Part III

The Tasks of Economic Theory in Solving the Problems of the Harmonious Development of Energy and Guidelines for their Solution

INTRODUCTORY REMARKS

In the previous section, we addressed the fundamental question of the main direction of harmonious progress, which is the mass introduction of RES technologies in all areas of power generation and transformation. In this section, we will discuss the theoretical issues that hinder and even block the wider use of RES technologies. Mainly, the market economy cannot avoid the disastrous effects of fossil fuel combustion on the environment to secure the supply and ensure the sufficiency of energy resources for future generations. Due to the existing stereotypes of the allegedly contradictory financial support for these resources, and despite their different environmental impacts, large-scale implementations of RES technologies are being prevented. As investors avoid costs that are not directly related to the operation of an individual investment project, they are passed onto the public in the form of air, water and land pollution. As a result, it causes serious consequences for people's health and well-being.

The use of RES technologies addresses these problems in a variety of ways, although there are quite serious economic and technical barriers that prevent us from receiving their major benefits compared to fossil fuels. The main struggle is that the use of RES technology is mostly associated with low-power plants, with the exception of wind farms. This means that energy flow management, which is essential for ensuring the security of the energy supply, becomes extremely challenging. Those who invest in energy generation capacity do not bear the costs of supply security and, therefore, it must be financially supported by the government. Support measures are the subject of a very controversial discussion—therefore, it is necessary to clearly define the economic rationale and the most appropriate measures in order to ensure the smooth penetration of RES technologies into the market, which, unfortunately, is dominated by fierce competition. It can be noted that capital-intensive measures aimed at ensuring the security of the energy supply achieve synergic effects only when addressing the Climate Change Programme's commitments at the same time. On the other hand, economic studies, conducted in a variety of countries, show the positive macroeconomic effect of the implementation of RES technologies. Therefore, the centre of gravity of these decisions shifts to state and municipal levels in terms of the formulation of a wise economic policy.

Based on the unified idea of energy advancement, I strive to substantiate the methodology for the harmonious environmental transformation of energy, by establishing the necessary theoretical solutions, methods, practical tools and assumptions.

CHAPTER ONE

THE USE OF RENEWABLE ENERGY RESOURCES AS A KEY DIRECTION FOR THE HARMONIOUS DEVELOPMENT OF ENERGY

The characterisation and classification of RES

a) RES utilisation in Lithuania

In 2016, in more than 30 countries around the world, renewable energy was cheaper than power manufactured using fossil fuel. Lithuania has not yet joined this squad. Michael Drexler, the head of the Infrastructure and Development Unit of Deutsche Bank, at the World Economic Forum, has stated that renewable energy has reached a breakthrough. Not only it is commercially viable, but also attractive to investors in the long run, as it guarantees a stable, inflation-protected return.

First of all, our main task is to define the object of the research, as the concept of RES is too broad, thus, it often obscures the essence, and might even lead to errors in economic policy. In the scope of this study, it is impossible to analyse all the possible types of RES, their application, potential implementation technologies and, especially, their utility. Also, the utilisation dynamics of each type of RES are different, given the lower cost of technology over time. Therefore, the initial goal is to move the debate and deliberations into a certain area defined by uniform rules and economic law, combining, as much as possible, a variety of different opinions.

In the case of RES, individual, non-systematic knowledge, which is often disseminated for purely promotional purposes, suppressing the negative consequences, can be particularly damaging. What is more, there is a diversity of views regarding the measurement of progress. For example, the number of vehicles per thousand inhabitants is considered an indicator of well-being, but it is clear that an uncontrolled increase of this indicator at the expense of old, barely suitable for use vehicles will lead to an increase in pollution, noise and nervous stress. From time to time, with the help of advertising, doubtful facts become unquestionable truths. For example, you might often hear someone saying: "there is no sun in Lithuania", or that environmental energy produced from geothermal sources or wind energy is too expensive to implement. While, at the same time, the incredibly increased use of biofuel is celebrated as the greatest achievement of all times.

The distribution of the use of different kinds of RES in Lithuania is very uneven. Biomass, which is used almost exclusively for heat production, is one of the most widely used types of RES. However, biomass (wood and wood waste) can only be somewhat considered a RES. Essentially, it is a locally produced fuel—a product of economic activity, specifically, forestry. What is more, this type of fuel is manufactured during the combustion process, which is only partly considered to cause a CO_2-neutral effect. Actually, it is complete nonsense, as the climate change reports clearly show that biofuel combustion causes the highest CO_2 emissions.

A lot of progress has been achieved from the use of wind power as well. Some of the fastest-growing types of RES are solid biomass and wood waste for heat and wind power for electricity manufacturing. The use of solar and geothermal energy has also been growing, although this growth is not significant in the context of the total energy needs of the whole country.

If solid biomass, wood and wood waste are treated as a renewable energy source, it can be stated that almost 84% of all RES is used for heat production in Lithuania. Approximately 11% of different RES (wind, solar, etc.) are used for the generation of electricity and approximately 5% is used in the transportation sector in the form of biofuels which are blended into petroleum products.

The most worrying situation is in the transport sector. In this area, it is hardly possible to expect a more significant breakthrough in the near future, bearing in mind the growth of the fleet in cities and other urban areas. This condition can be called a natural disaster, as it has significantly worsened the quality of life in cities during recent decades due to heavy traffic and intolerable pollution.

Incorporating advanced technologies, we define particular ideas that can positively influence the harmonious progress of energy and sustainable energy development. However, this statement acquires meaning and content in a much broader organisational context (not on the basis of individual opinions), meaning that not the individual aspects, but the organised and structured body of knowledge determines the correct management of the process. The specificity of RES allows us to evaluate progress over a long transition period.

b) Classification of RES technologies

The ability to renew, as a distinguishing feature of RES, is the essential criteria for their classification. There are three main types of RES.

The first and most important aspect is the classification of RES on the basis of the nature of the renewables, their suitability and sufficiency for future use and the implementation of the corresponding economic measures. In the assessment of many theoretical and practical phenomena related to the use of RES, a classification based on the nature of source regeneration has been suggested and clearly defined as separating different types of RES:

- **Natural renewal properties**, referring to the infinity of natural RES—wind, solar, geothermal energy—which is one of the main points of sustainable energy development in order to ensure a supply of energy for future generations. RES technologies are naturally occurring phenomena which can eventually, but only gradually, replace depleting forms of energy such as oil and gas. The wind, the sun, and geothermal energy represent the absolutely natural, infinite phenomenon of regeneration, the economic evaluation of which is still not properly understood and validated in economic theory. This type of energy does not need to be produced and will last for many centuries, so the extent of its utilisation during one period does not affect the extent of its utilisation in another period and, consequently, does not affect the expectations of policymakers, investors and consumers.
- **Renewal as a product of more or less continuous economic activity.** This is represented by the biofuels, the produce of forestry and agricultural activities. Their relative renewal properties depend on the continuity of economic activity. Currently, the greatest hopes are related to the use of biomass for heat production. However, the widespread use of products from economic activities might have a huge impact on the decline and deterioration of national assets—forests and land. The use of biofuels is particularly controversial, especially bearing in mind their actual pollution which is generated during the combustion process.
- **Recovery, as a continuous process of waste generation.** This is most prominently represented by municipal, agricultural and livestock waste, the stable accumulation of which is conditionally referred to as regeneration, which allows the utilisation of this waste for energy purposes. Reusability of this waste is directly related to a positive environmental effect. By using RES technologies, waste recovery is a good tool for solving environmental and global climate change problems. However, the adaptation for energy purposes is quite limited in this case.

The latest example of such type of renewability is Fortum Klaipeda Combined Heat and Power Plant—a new, modern, municipal waste-to-energy cogeneration plant, which is currently operating at a very competitive level, due to the paid utilisation services of municipal waste.

In Fig. 3-1., a schematic diagram of the classification of RES is presented.

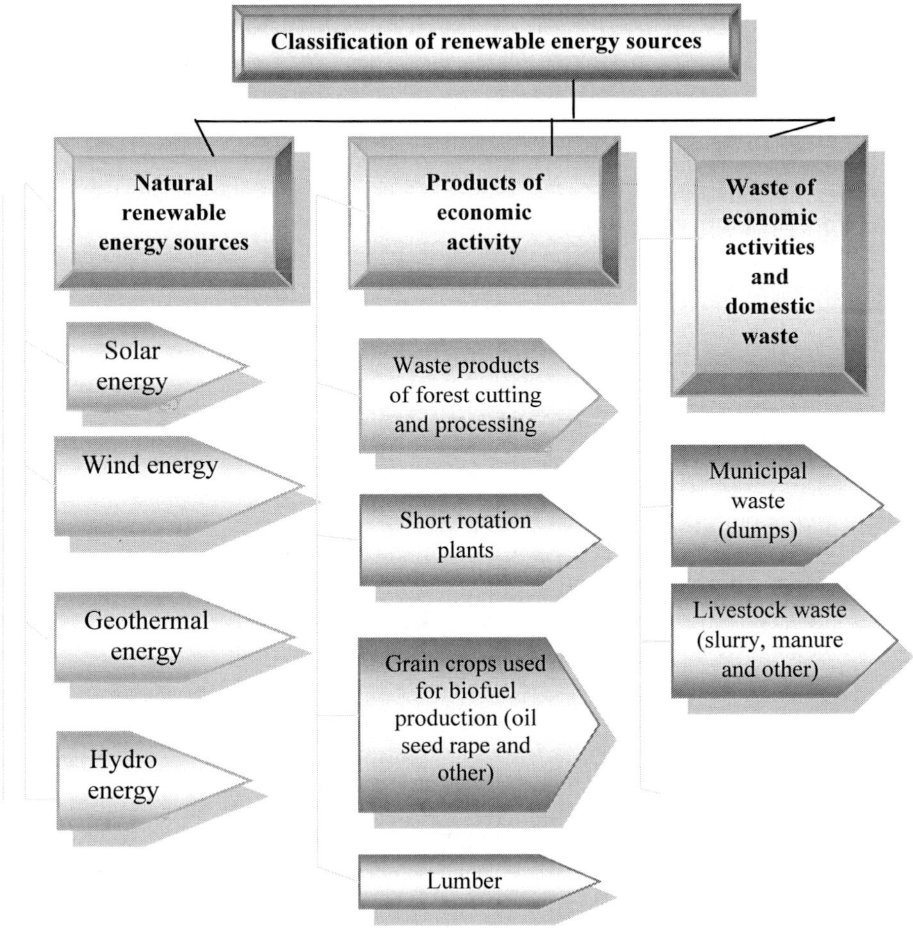

Fig. 3-1. Schematic diagram of the classification of RES

Regarding the nature of resource regeneration, two different regeneration types have to be distinguished: natural sources of energy—solar, wind and environmental energy (earth, air, water) are eternal, inexhaustible and should, therefore, be given a different name, e.g. eternal or natural. Renewal through all other energy sources depends on economic activity. Therefore, the assessment of the problem of economic expectations differs significantly depending on the nature of the recovery and this should be clearly reflected in the economic policy. What is more, it would justify the financial support of particular types of resources.

When all types of RES are labelled as equal, biomass is interpreted as a more reliable energy source than solar energy, without considering the natural reliability of different types of RES. Economists' research over the past decade convinces us that expectations play a key role in defining key macroeconomic phenomena and their fluctuations. It means that future expectations, contrary to the example of fossil fuel or biofuel, are not less in extent than current needs, which has a direct effect on investments. The use of natural RES is widely recognised as essential to the development of sustainable patterns of energy use, as well as a way of addressing the challenges of future energy supply. It is noteworthy that investor expectations have led to the emergence of new financial channels and the use of innovative instruments for end-user financing.

However, serious problems and economic policy errors at state level still exist. In the case of renewable energy, there is a misguided, univocal approach, treating all kinds of RES as a whole, allowing a comparison of biofuels and solar energy as competing forms of energy and, consequently, attributing an unquestionable advantage to biofuels. However, the attitude of the state and municipalities must be different from the short-term individual assessment, because the true value of RES is reflected in their diversity and customisation. It should be noted that when comparing RES, they mainly differ in one essential respect. Solar, wind and geothermal energy represent the natural, infinite, eternal, non-generated regeneration phenomenon, the economic evaluation of which has to be based on economic regularity. This regularity denies one of the fundamental laws of the economy, which declares that as demand increases, the price of a commodity increases as well. This is true for virtually all fossil fuels and biofuels. In contrast, it is the opposite for natural RES—the higher the demand, the more energy is produced, and the more the price of energy created using natural RES drops.

Solar energy development was greatly influenced not only by financial support mechanisms but also by the fall of the price of solar photovoltaic cells, which since 1977 has decreased more than 100 times. This is clearly demonstrated in Fig. 3-2.

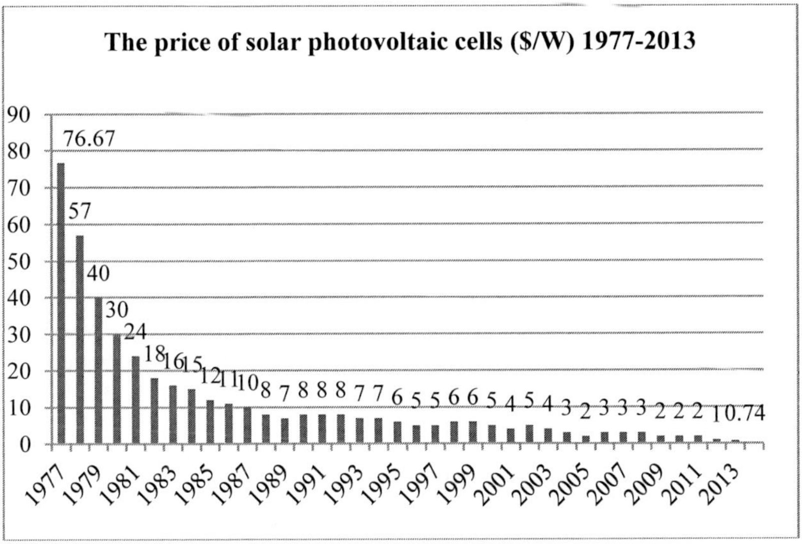

Fig. 3-2. Price Dynamics of Solar Photovoltaic Cells ($ / W) 1977-2013 (Bloomberg 2014)

Gross domestic consumption of solar photovoltaic electricity (2005-2014) varies greatly in different European countries. Lithuania's neighbour countries, Estonia and Latvia, do not use solar photovoltaic technology. Neither does Norway, which produces its electricity with the use of hydropower, nor Iceland, basing its energy production needs on geothermal energy. In 2014, solar power was most widely used in Germany (3100 toe) and Italy (1918 toe), while the following European countries have used solar power to a smaller degree: Spain – 707 toe, France – 508 toe, the United Kingdom – 348 toe, and Greece – 326 toe. The extent of solar electricity consumption in the United Kingdom is close to the use of solar power usage in southern European countries. This fact perfectly illustrates that solar energy can be successfully implemented and used in northern European countries.

Meanwhile, biomass is a product of an economic activity that can only be partially described as renewable. At present, the most harmful is the short-sighted policy of promoting biofuels which has given the green light to mass deforestation. Looking at the forest as a raw material for fuel production, tremendous damage can be caused to its natural biodiversity as well as to the whole of society. There is a definite lack of knowledge and research in this area—this is the main rationale for such a huge increase in demand for forest material portrayed as fuel. No studies are assessing the impact of the use of trees on biodiversity in Lithuania, and the biodiversity of national forests itself is also poorly researched and known. National parks order nature studies in their areas, but data on wild forests is only fragmentary and episodic, usually limited to the search for rare species. Therefore, the only studies to rely on are the works of foreign authors.

The concept of energy progress in the context of energy as a whole

It is difficult to evaluate the direction and feasibility of harmonious progress in energy, separating it from the whole entirety of energetics. As stated by Schelling (1995), "concepts can never be defined in isolation, and they are only truly scientifically proven when they are associated with the whole". The previous chapters underline the key objective of energy progress—the implementation of the Climate Change Programme using RES as a means to achieve it. Such an approach to energy advancement must be based on a methodology for overcoming theoretical and practical challenges in achieving a harmonious environment for energy advancement and shift in the human mindset, as well as including specialist training in the mass deployment of RES technologies.

In terms of harmonious energy progress, it is necessary to define the subject matter itself. The concept of sustainable development defines the basic principles of how sustainable energy development is perceived. However, in order to understand what the energy progress actually means and how it can be interpreted in relation to a particular country, it is necessary to look at its whole complexity.

But first, we must choose an energy research base that covers the whole entirety, as we are talking about aspects that are difficult to evaluate economically. Therefore, we are guided by actual, time-tested methodological tools that allow us to express our country's energy mix. Energetics is a sector of the economy whose "commodity" is unique in the sense that energy can be subdivided into physical units, e.g. joules (J), kilowatt-hours (kWh), tonnes of oil equivalent (toe), and so on. This has enabled the development of such a methodical tool—a fuel-based comprehensive analysis of energy production, transformation and consumption. This is the country's fuel and energy balance which describes the country's internal fuel and energy resources, their production, imports, exports, inventory change, energy consumption for electricity and heat production, reprocessing, non-energy use, transportation and distribution losses, and cost to end-users. The fuel-energy balance is a practical, internationally approved, legally valid statistical method of estimating and analysing the country's energy mix. It provides a lot of information about any country, i.e., it allows us to evaluate the energy situation in Lithuania comparing it with other countries' energy development estimates. Fig. 3-3. provides a different type of fuel and energy scheme—a generalised structure of primary and secondary energies, which allows us to envision the object and direction of the research more clearly. The analysis would allow the whole energy sector to be covered, including the consumption sphere. In the near future, and even today, energy consumers must become energy producing consumers. This is a very important moment because the main direction of energy transformation is the massive use of RES. More importantly, each type of primary and secondary local or imported energy (such as electricity or gasoline) has a definite scope of use and interchangeability. Thus, different types of fuel and energy occupy different positions in the fuel and energy flow scheme as seen in Fig. 3-3.

In this context, it is possible to visualise what constitutes the direction of energy advancement in technological terms. The main energy sources are solar, wind and environmental energy.

1. Imported electricity
2. Use of waste energy
3. Energy savings (e.g. home renovation)
4. Solid biomass, wood, wood waste
5. Biofuels
6. Biogas
7. Electricity for transport and hydrogen

During the transitional period, natural gas (that is currently undervalued) should be used for electricity generation and transport.

Progress in the sector of energetics can be understood when evaluating its entirety, bearing in mind that consumers are also a valuable part of it. Cities and settlements also need to be treated as consumers, in order to develop a fully-fledged RES policy in economic and organisational terms. The essence of the harmonious progress of energy must be expressed in the theses, reflecting its essential goals:

In order to define the purpose and the tasks of harmonious progress, we must first understand what this means for the whole country's economy. The country's economy is a structured organisational entity of the state. Therefore, energy resources should be treated not only on the basis of technology but also in terms of the extraction (or import), supply, transformation and final consumption. The smooth functioning of energy affects all areas of life—therefore, it is important to define the essence of the approach and design many aspects on a unanimous methodological basis. In many respects, public expenditure relates to the expenditure that is not normally evaluated at the macroeconomic level.

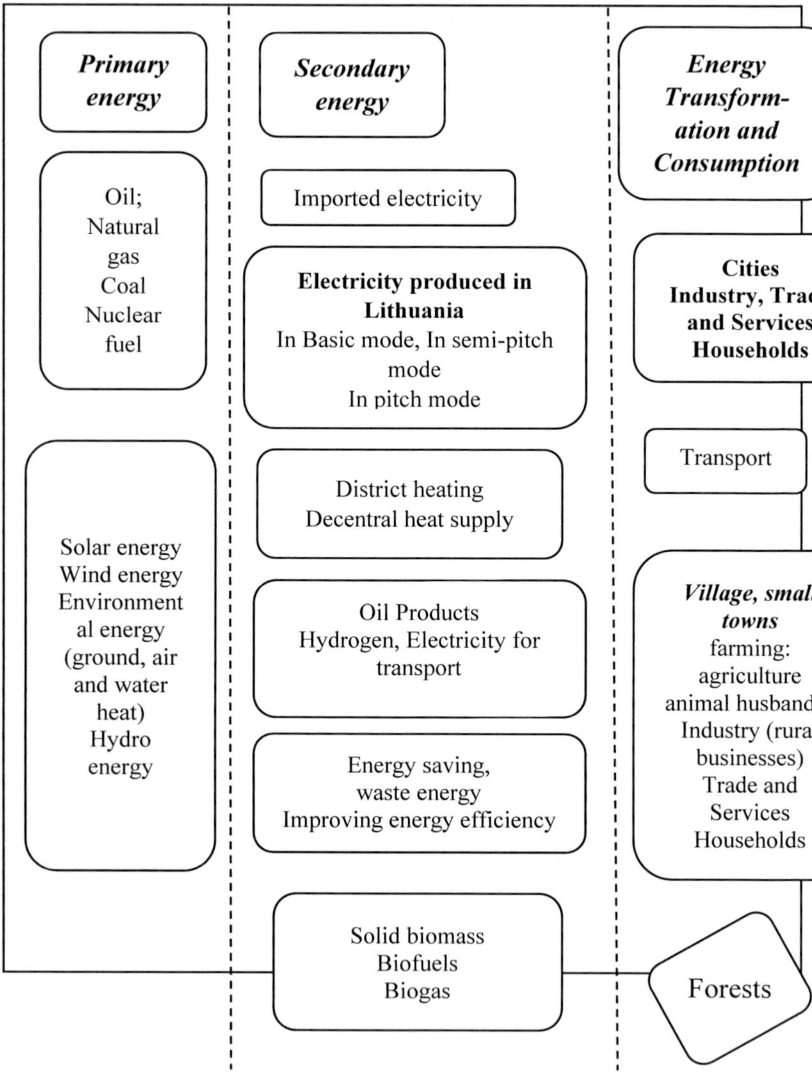

Fig. 3-3. Simplified scheme of types of fuel and energy, their transformation and demand

CHAPTER TWO

THE CONCEPT OF RES UTILISATION EFFICIENCY AND ITS CONTENT

General performance characteristics of RES

The new Lithuanian Energy Strategy, approved by the Government of the Republic of Lithuania, marks a purposeful change in energy policy towards energy independence through the adoption of RES and increasing energy efficiency. This demonstrates the ambition to join western electricity and gas systems. Increasing the production of energy from renewable sources is one of the key directions of this strategy. It is estimated that by 2030, 45% of total energy consumption will come from RES; energy from renewable and other clean sources will account for as much as 80% of the total energy consumption. In order to achieve the strategic objectives, it is necessary to promote the active involvement of energy users in the energy production process. Citizens who choose to become energy consumers will be encouraged to produce their own energy from renewable sources. However, the question remains how such ambitious goals will be achieved. It is clear that technological advancement focuses on the development of RES, concentrating on energy saving as an alternative to energy use as well as promoting decentralised energy production, enabling energy users to become energy suppliers through smart technologies. This results in a wider dissemination of knowledge to different groups of the population and a significant increase in the need for appropriately trained professionals. Therefore, it can be noted that many factors make it necessary to find an adequate methodological tool for emerging problems, which relates to the development of the knowledge-based economy.

The main problem is the scientific justification of the need to generalise and structure the knowledge about the usefulness of RES so that the uptake of RES technologies can bring maximum benefit to society. It is essential to theoretically demonstrate the importance of unifying an organisational system of sustainable thinking in education and policy organisation. Also, it is necessary to define the potential public role of municipalities, where the effect of RES use manifests in practice, and to present a generalised analysis of the situation.

Theoretical work is summarised, and the analysis of the origins of the knowledge economy theory is presented, demonstrating the efficiency and uniqueness of knowledge as a factor in production, and linking the uniqueness of knowledge and RES in terms of economic regularities. Also, the support measures aimed at the dissemination of knowledge about the usefulness of RES and the social, environmental, macroeconomic effects achieved with the introduction of such technologies, as well as the organisational preconditions for the dissemination of knowledge, are being investigated.

Bearing in mind that the public benefits of the uptake of RES technologies are unquestionable and almost universally recognised, there is only a need to evaluate these benefits and provide a cost-benefit analysis that would show the value of supporting RES technologies. Theoretically, it is possible, but in practice, it is a challenging task to achieve. In theory, not all benefits of using RES are fully quantifiable. The total value of RES consists of the direct benefit as a result of the produced energy, plus the social benefit gained by society in various different ways. This is why, from the knowledge economy point of view, the concept of support measures for RES has to be organised and managed, taking into consideration all the benefits gained in the long-term perspective. The support system depends on the added value created throughout the whole chain of provision and consumption, defining the objective distribution of revenue and costs.

Abstract theoretical definitions become meaningful only when they come to life. To achieve this goal, several years of consistent work have been done. This is reflected in the publications of Klevienė (2011) and Klevienė, Murauskaitė and Klevas (2017), where the interconnections between knowledge and RES as well as the prerequisites for the widespread use of RES are discussed. RES and energy efficiency topics have become highly popular after the launch of European Commission directives (European Commission 2009); (European Commission 2010); (European Commission 2012). In Lithuania, these directives were noticeable in the launch of various laws. In order to ensure successful implementation of these laws and directives, it must be clear for the whole of society, at the level of individuals as well as politicians, why it is necessary to support RES technologies.

Another especially important issue is the evaluation of direct and indirect value caused by RES. Fig. 3-4 shows the generalised usefulness of RES at both national and individual levels.

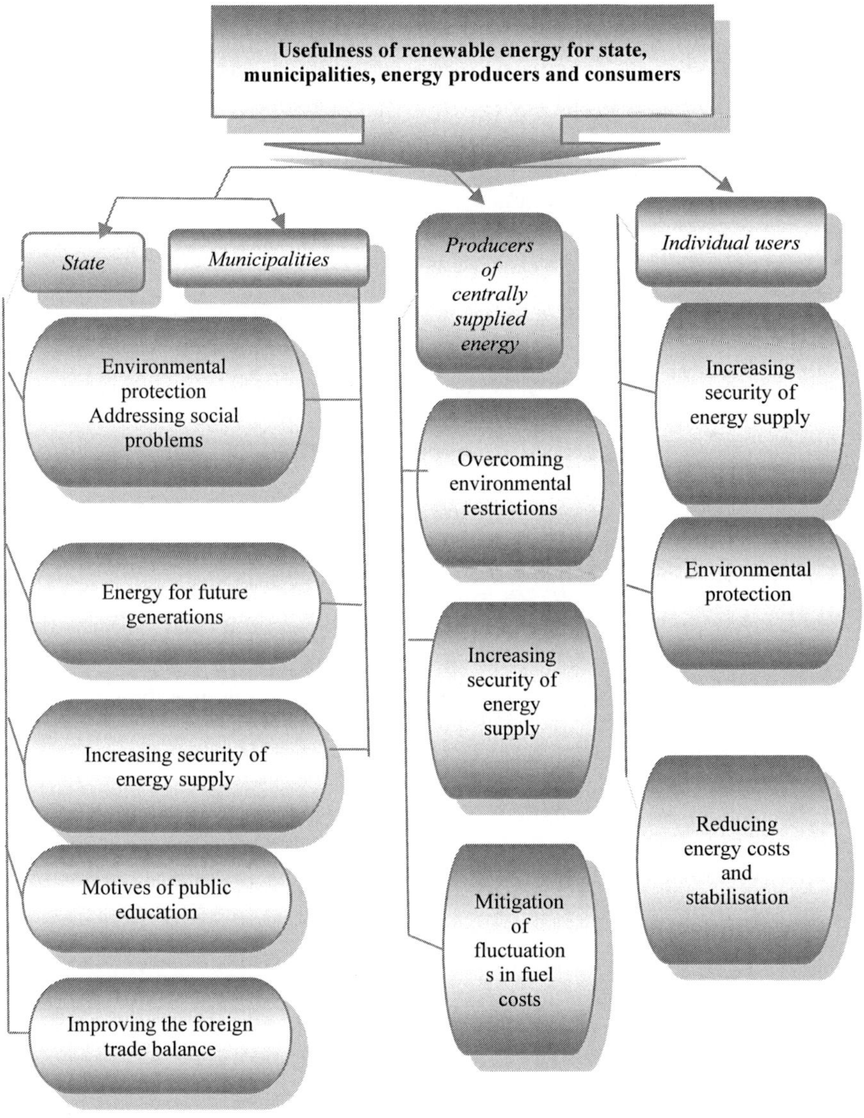

Fig. 3-4. The usefulness of RES from the users' perspectives

The most difficult part is defining who is in receipt of a positive effect and who has to organise the implementation of the positive effect accordingly. This requires identifying the external positive effects of the RES projects in regional policies and summarising these effects as an overall contribution. This is possible and things are currently shifting in this direction, but not in an organised and targeted way, as this issue is often not considered as important as practical action. Research into the influence of RES on macroeconomic indicators has been ongoing for several years, but it remains mainly visible only among the scientific community.

First and foremost, an approach is needed which reveals the principles behind the evaluation method and the basis on which RES technologies should be supported. The following theoretical approaches are based on the concept of the knowledge economy:

- Public and private market participants' support for the RES business is seen as a remedy for market failures when addressing sustainable development (Brown 2001).
- Prices for all energy sources must be based on social costs, assuming that all aspects of energy and fuel use—reliability, environmental, social and renewable—are methodologically feasible.
- The usefulness of RES can be measured in terms of real benefits now and in the future, which are not captured in the justification of investment efficiency. The approach to addressing this problem and integrating energy projects into the regional development process are discussed in the works of Klevas (2015), and Klevas and Antinucci (2004).
- The justification for the promotion of RES is based on a comparison of using all fuels and energy sources available in the energy system, and assessing their competitiveness according to various aspects of sustainable development.

The methodological principle of the economic evaluation of the external utility

From the point of view of the concept of the knowledge economy, a particular feature of market errors is the insufficient dissemination of knowledge and information to individual consumers, who also have the potential to become energy suppliers. This is particularly important for the use of natural RES, i.e. solar, wind, geothermal and aerothermal energy, as these technologies (except wind power) are generally low-powered and are still referred to in the scientific literature as producing users.

Economic theory explains the fundamental reason why there is a lack of demand for certain goods and services on the market (even though they are highly beneficial to society). The main reason is that the external benefits generated by the good or service are not reflected in the direct market operations and, thus, in the price (Klevas 2010). In the case of RES, this is a crucial moment. The external environmental benefits initiated by the use of RES could be the best example of external value. The use of RES reduces negative environmental effects, saves organic fuel resources and helps to assimilate new technologies. Demand for RES in the market does not reflect the previously mentioned public benefit caused by the use of energy made from renewable sources. The benefits are scattered among various users: individuals, future generations, cities, companies, etc. Even people who do not participate in the transactions of this market can sometimes get a free share of the benefits.

If the external benefits associated with the use of green energy are unknown or simply underestimated, consumers will choose the amount of energy they purchase according to the demand curve. Usually, the amount of green electricity will be much smaller than would be economically justified. However, by purchasing so-called "green" electricity produced from RES, consumers help to reduce environmental pollution, and this benefit can be evaluated by the general public in the form of preventing diseases and other negative consequences that are caused by environmental pollution. These benefits are not reflected in the demand curve. As a result, the price stabilises at a lower point than it would have if the actual efficiency of the green energy had been estimated. The demand curve should be in a position where this external benefit is estimated. The main issue that needs to be achieved is including all these benefits in the expression of economic indicators. As a result, the volume of RES production could be sold at a much higher price.

We note that benefits can be known and declared, but that knowledge is not transformed into concrete practical tools in the form of calculations. However, the amount of convincing calculations is not enough either. Much larger structural changes are needed to start the uptake of RES, and even more so for it to become mass-scale. Therefore, knowledge becomes the main driver in this process.

In conclusion, it can be stated that the individual consumer does not receive the mentioned benefits directly, or it is difficult to evaluate the actual benefits in the short-term, therefore, municipalities, as collective purchasers and, thus, beneficiaries, are responsible for organising the demand.

In economic theory, the market's inability to assess the external benefits generated is a particular problem (Čiegis 2004).

The increase in social benefit which arises due to the implementation of RES, increased energy efficiency and energy savings is illustrated in the article by Jenniches and Worrell (2019). It presents the results of an investigation into regional, economic and environmental impacts of renewable energy developments in the Aachen region. After the evaluation, the excess amount of social benefit can become a basis for tax advantages, directed at increasing energy efficiency, savings and further implementation of RES in general.

> The energy transition is a challenge that affects regions on various scales. This paper presents the economic chances of deploying the renewable energy technology solar photovoltaic in a German region. Total regional economic effects of 280 PV plants, installed in 2014 with a cumulative capacity of 3.7 MW, lead to a regional value-added of approximately €3.8 million (€1019/kW installed, €57/MWh electricity generated) and employment effects of 42 full-time person-years (11 person-years/MW installed), occurring from 2014 to 2034. The avoided 0.7 greenhouse gas emissions of these plants are 2365 tons CO_2 equivalents per year ($kgCO_2$-eq/kWh generated) and the avoided air pollution is 0.97 tSO_2 per year, 1.48 tNO_x per year, and 0.07 t NMVOCs per year in 2014. The total economic effects of regional value-added, avoided CO_2 emissions, and avoided air pollution per year in 2014 range from €0.8 million-€1 million or (€208–€277 per kW installed, €231–€307 per MWh electricity generated) (Jenniches and Worrell 2019).

In order to evaluate the project efficiency of any type of fuel, e.g. gas or RES, at an individual project or country level, it is essential to conduct an extended economic analysis. This should be supplemented by environmental indicators that measure the environmental impact of gas or RES project implementation or evaluate the external costs of energy production. The main parameter influencing the external expenditure of electricity production is the emission of pollutants into the atmosphere. By estimating the amount of damage caused by major atmospheric pollutant emissions and transferring it into monetary units, the cost of external power generation can be calculated, which adds ecological indicators to the classic cost-benefit analysis. An ecological indicator would, in fact, show that renewable energy projects are more efficient than those of traditional energy sources, despite the significant capital investment needed to implement them. The economic value of the investment project can, therefore, be defined as the total value of the project's investment, operating costs and revenues, taking into account transfer payments (taxes, subsidies, write-offs, tax credits) and external costs.

CHAPTER THREE

THE ESSENCE OF THE ENERGY SUPPLY RELIABILITY ESTIMATION PROBLEM IN ECONOMIC THEORY

General issues regarding the security of the energy supply

The most important aspect of energy development in the RES market is the accusation of unreliability. Reliability could be defined as the availability of using energy in its various forms, at any time, in sufficient quantities and at reasonable prices. At the macroeconomic level, the country's reliability regarding its energy supply is measured by the net dependence on imports, the share of local energy and RES in the primary energy, and electricity balances.

In researching these problems, it is important not to confuse the concepts of technical reliability and security of supply. The security of the energy supply is linked to the provision of strategically important energy sources—oil and natural gas. The oil and gas sectors are vital arteries that fuel Lithuania's energy supply. Disruptions in supply, shortages of supply and fluctuations in oil and gas prices can have serious consequences, not only for energy companies but for the economy as a whole.

Egenhofer (2004) defines the security of energy supply as the physical sufficiency of supply to meet energy needs at a given energy price. Thus, the problem of the security of supply involves quantitative risks and price risks.

Power interruptions can be defined as a drop in physical energy supply below a certain level or threshold (for a sufficiently long period) or when the price of energy reaches a certain level or threshold, or when both cases happen at once.

Uncertainty of supply arises in the event of the physical disruption of the energy supply or in the event of severe price fluctuations (Lockwood 1997). This is in line with the definition of energy security of the International Energy Agency (IEA), defined as the security of energy supply at moderate energy prices.

With regard to the issue of energy and fuel security and its economic interpretation, it needs to be assessed in a structured way, not only on the basis of the physical characteristics of the fuel itself but also on the country-specific situation. In this respect, here is the definition of the situation in Lithuania:

a) Physical links to the oil, gas and electricity networks to supply oil and gas (in this case, exports and imports) were physically connected to one country—Russia. Currently, the Liquefied Natural Gas (LNG) terminal has diversified the supply of natural gas, which has significantly improved the energy security and reliability situation.

b) Dependence on global oil price volatility, which can be extreme (e.g. in 2008), also causes gas prices to rise (with a delay of half a year). After the closure of the nuclear power plant, the problem of the security of the oil and gas supply also directly affected the power generation sector.

Real social costs of an unreliable oil and gas supply are not reflected in the price of oil and gas. The global oil price, as well as the gas price dependence on oil fluctuations, are "indifferent" to the country's reliability problems. A rational way to estimate the cost of interruptions in imported fuel as an economic factor would be to introduce a separate tax on unsafe (unreliable) oil and gas supplies. This tax would accumulate funds to manage unreliable oil and gas supplies, particularly for the construction of storage facilities. However, in order to determine the optimal level of such a tax, or at least to calculate the potential costs that may result from a supply disruption, information is needed regarding: (a) the marginal loss function, (b) marginal reliability (or control) costs, and (c) administrative costs. Determining such a mark-up is feasible and methodologically correct with respect to economic theory.

Smart grid technologies in district heating and power grid systems

a) Smart grids in the heat sector

The energy reliability problem can be solved with smart grid technologies. With the adoption of the Energy Efficiency Directive by the European Commission at the end of 2012, new requirements for heat suppliers have become evident. Article 7 of the Directive states that from 1 January 2015, energy suppliers will have to save 1.5% of the annual energy sales to the end-users. The directive stipulates that DH customers in multi-apartment buildings must be provided with individual heat meters that reflect actual energy consumption, as only consumers have the means to control their own consumption in DH. Where individual heat accounting in apartments is not appropriate (due to high cost or other reasons) each heater must be equipped with heat distributors. According to EU requirements, 80% of all electricity consumers must be equipped with smart meters by 2020.

1. One of the most important components of smart grids is smart and comprehensive energy metering, so this provision of the directive would speed up the development of smart CHDs.

2. Another important part of smart networks, including DH networks, is the optimal planning and management of energy flows and the centralised planning of the energy, waste energy (waste heat from industrial and agricultural companies) and waste streams.

Optimal energy flow planning is the basis for the efficient use of local energy resources, which promotes the development of conventional and low cogeneration, increases the use of renewable resources and waste streams, and promotes the development of DH and cooling in densely built-up areas, cities and densely populated areas. Optimal planning and management of energy resources and flows of generated energy are conducive to the economic development of the region and enable the development of an advanced energy economy that best meets the sustainability criteria.

3. The third important part of smart DH is the ability to connect several heat producers or suppliers to the DH network.

Taking into account the cost of energy resources used for heat production, we can model DH development scenarios according to the criteria of economic efficiency.

Combined DH and cooling systems are featured both in the 35th Congress of the District Power Supply and in reports prepared by Graz Technical University researchers, as well as other scientific institutions and DH companies. Such systems integrate solar energy-absorbing equipment into DH networks, test seasonal heat accumulation, and create smart heat supply networks using IT technologies.

4. The fourth important aspect of smart DHs is the ability to (re)store the heat that has been produced.

Heat storage technologies include:

- Power to gas (P2G) technology
- High capacity batteries
- Underground (geothermal) storage facilities of thermal energy
- Artificial water pools, dams—as large-scale heat accumulators
- Compressed air energy storage
- Flying wheels
- Electrolysis

- Geothermal heat storage and heat supply technologies
- Other technologies.

Energy flows in summer (e.g. July) and winter (e.g. January) are totally different, therefore, due to the specificity of solar energy, its potential is limited depending on the season. Solar collectors generate high amounts of energy during the summer months (e.g. July), while consumers' heat demand is low, as heat is only used to produce hot water. Most of the excess energy (approx. 82%) is transferred/diverted to underground geothermal heat storage. During winter months (e.g. January), approximately 25% of the required energy is generated by solar collectors, half of the required energy is supplied from a thermal underground energy storage facility, and the remaining part (about 25%) is produced by gas boilers.

The great example would be the heating technology of 52 homes built in Drake Landing Solar Community, Okotoks, Alberta, Canada, using 52 solar panels based on the solar thermal method, where each house was equipped with solar panels with a capacity of 1.5MW. Each house was also equipped with an autonomous heat storage tank and one common heat storage tank, which was installed underground in specially drilled shafts using geothermal energy principles (144 boreholes, 7 m deep, occupying 35 m^2 of land). The ground in the borehole warms up to 800 °C in late summer. Thermal insulation, clay, and the moisture-proof coating was used to reduce heat loss from wells. This thermal energy storage was designed to hold the stored heat during the non-heating season, i.e. in the summer.

Thermal energy was used for heating and hot water production. During the winter, the heat circulated in a small circle, using local heat tanks installed in individual homes without supplying heat to the underground heat storage system. During the summer, autonomous boilers were closed, and all heat was transferred to an underground thermal energy storage facility. In this heating system, each individual home is both a consumer and a producer of heat, therefore, the system can be considered smart and capable of producing more energy than it needs. For storing the excess energy, there was an underground storage area that transmitted the accumulated heat to DH in the winter months.

Other smart centralised network development projects

Industrial, agricultural and other companies often generate additional, waste energy that can be used in production or transferred to DH networks. In densely built-up areas with industrial or other types of companies that are connected to a centralised heating network, it is possible to combine the capacities of industrial and DH companies by supplying (transferring or selling) waste energy to DH networks. For example, in Austria and Germany, cooperation between manufacturing and DH companies is being promoted in order to use waste energy more efficiently. In Austria, the development of technologies used for vegetable and other biomass energy production has been initiated. Therefore, the experience and cooperation projects of local authorities, businesses, local communities and heat consumers in Austria can be useful for the development of DH network projects in Lithuanian regions (link: http://www.biomassehof-stmk.at). The practical application of waste energy utilisation capabilities depends on the ability to manage and distribute thermal energy in DH networks. This opportunity arises with the introduction of computerised, automatic systems, otherwise known as smart DH network management technology. Smart DH networks operate in a similar way to electricity smart grids, although they are not so flexible. A smart centralised network can not only supply heat (in winter) but also condition the area (in summer). However, management of the heat network is a much more complicated task, requiring much bigger investments.

The smart DH technology works locally, i.e. in areas that are connected into a DH system. What is more, the development possibilities in areas that are economically beneficial to the DH system should be considered. The use of smart technologies is limited by the amount of energy supplied and consumed. Smart DH network technology cannot be imagined without the application of heat storage technology. In larger cities, where the DH network is dense and the DH companies have more customers, thermal energy is stored in large-capacity boilers, where fossil energy sources are mainly used to maintain the temperature. In smaller towns or when developing the DH system in remote areas, or in case of the expansion of DH to other settlements, the storage of thermal energy is solved by using solar energy—particularly, solar panels—to generate and store additional heat.

The development of smart technologies in DH companies has the following advantages:

- Various types of fuels can be combined for use in heat production, without the necessity of using fossil fuels.
- Synergies between fuels used to produce thermal energy are possible.
- Ability to use many different types of fuels.
- Possibility to connect, manage and control many manufacturers into DH networks.
- Possibility to securely store and manage thermal energy.

Smart grids (both electricity and heat) are built using existing infrastructure, i.e. using the same networks of electricity and heat. However, the whole management system, data transmission, information exchange, security system and energy storage infrastructure (storage, tanks, etc.) is being developed from scratch.

Advantages of using smart networks:
1. Technological innovation and novelty
2. Ability to regulate, analyse, manage, control and monitor energy flows
3. Reduction and control of pollutant emissions
4. More efficient use of energy resources
5. Encouraged development of energy storage technologies
6. Encouraged use of different forms of energy
7. Promotion of RES

Disadvantages of using smart networks:
1. Need for significant investment
2. Difficult integration with existing infrastructure
3. Insufficient number of users increases the return on investment period or hinders the development of smart grid technologies

Technologically, the development of the heat network is limited by physical-technical indicators. A DH network is a local system with quite a small and simple system and a relatively low number of users. Electric networks, meanwhile, are much more widespread. Smart technologies are not constrained by physical factors. Therefore, smart technologies can be deployed at regional and national levels, across multiple countries, across Europe, or even through the development of trans-regional smart grids.

b) Use of smart networks and automation tools in power energetics

There is a lack of research and practical examples of smart DH systems compared to smart grid technologies. At present and in the future, smart grid technologies are and will be the most important element when installing and using various autonomous wind, solar and geothermal power plants.

In order to ensure the reliability of the Lithuanian electricity supply, it is planned to create interconnections between the electricity systems of the Baltic States and the EU. The government ordered the Lithuanian electricity transmission system operator, Litgrid, to implement this project by 2020. Lithuania will become an equal participant in the common European electricity market and part of the system management. In order to ensure the reliability and security of services, in the next decade, the entire distribution network is planned to be modernised and a smart network created. This project is expected to receive $1.7 billion of support and be finished by 2025. A total of 34 million euros of this amount will be invested in seven smart grid projects, the main ones being pilot projects on network automation, smart meters, the implementation of a unified dispatch centre and a distribution network management system. The funds will also be used to connect new users and to invest in IT systems as well as other tools.

A smart grid is a power grid, upgraded with digital technology, dedicated to the transmission of power from the producer to the purchaser. It creates a mutual interconnection between manufacturer and buyer that controls the appliances in the consumer's home in order to save power, reduce electricity costs, and improve power quality and transmission reliability.

The concept of smart grid technologies includes a communication infrastructure (interconnected, remotely controlled network elements communicating their status), smart meters (information on the electricity quality and consumption, receiving of control signals, providing information for the user), automated network management (consumer management systems, GIS, distribution management systems, etc.), customer service, and information systems.

The main features of a smart grid are: receiving and managing all generation sources; power flow—both from the network to the users and to the network from the consumer devices ("consumer" means an active participant in the energy supply chain); a developed and liberal market; a variety of tariffs; real-time electricity billing; a self-healing network; optimal asset management; as well as easy and transparent identification of technological and commercial losses.

The benefits of a smart grid will affect the energy sector, the state and the consumer. A smart grid will increase the efficiency of power generation by approximately 10% through lower grid support costs, straightening of the consumption curve, lower commercial and technological losses, and more targeted investment. It will provide appropriate service quality, together with information and solutions for efficient electricity consumption and production: higher quality (reduction of frequency and duration of faults, voltage fluctuations), measures for more efficient use and saving, electricity trading (micro-generation), and new services based on the existing infrastructure. It will allow the formation of an integrated, secure, reliable and efficient electricity system in the EU: tools for integration into EU networks, increasing the security of the electricity supply, reduction of

CO_2, increased attractiveness for investments in the country, and economic growth. The expected results of smart grid benefits are: a 10% reduction in the tariff's component of generation and distribution, up to 10% savings on bills, solutions for hourly accounting and price signalling solutions, peak usage reduced by 5%, off-peak usage increased by 10%, and 20% off the electricity demand generated by consumers.

There are good smart accounting practices in other countries. For example, Ireland has had a 2.5% drop in consumption, and an 8.8% drop in peak, and France reduced its peak by 1.5% (2010), and then 2.5% (2011). According to the "VaasaETT" report, the results for various markets vary: 5.1%-8.7% drop in consumption, 5%-16% drop in peak.

The influence of smart grids on wind power plants is unequivocal. Wind volatility cannot guarantee a steady supply of electricity and energy independence—therefore, the problem of electricity balance arises. However, thanks to the use of smart grids and the interconnection of the electricity grid with the grid of the whole EU, wind farms will be able to make a significant contribution to overall electricity production. Smart grids on low-power wind farms allow us to notice network malfunctions, balance household needs and reduce electricity costs. The influence of smart grids on various low-power RES plants will increase unequivocally. Due to the use of smart grids in the urban infrastructure, the ambient air quality will improve, which will significantly contribute to the objectives of the Paris Agreement.

Methodological principles of the evaluation of energy resource regeneration

The dynamic criterion of the distribution of energy resources opens up new perspectives for the development of theories that are associated with solving major economic problems (Griffin and Steel, 1986). The fundamental difference between the dynamic and the static criteria is determined by the immanent quality of renewable and non-renewable energy resources, the fact that one period is economically different from one another, plus the fact that the use of resources in one period affects their future use in another. Thus, the use of non-RES has economic consequences that need to be considered when making investment decisions. For example, an oilfield is depleted during an operation, which means that the owner is forced to decide to what extent he needs to delay oil recovery. Thus, one period is not economically identical to another. This issue can be expanded to a global, universal issue: today, current consumption is reducing the exhaustive resources for future consumption (absolutely, not relatively). Therefore, both the owner and the user of the water bodies, and, ultimately, society, must optimise both production and consumption. In terms of economic theory, there is a serious problem in terms of solving the dilemma of how to economically evaluate this aspect. As the dominant forms of energy—oil, natural gas, coal, uranium—are exhaustive, understanding the concept of a dynamic criterion can, in economic theory, help solve the problem of evaluating the advantages of RES.

The discounting. As discounting plays a crucial role in economic policy, and a statement of its magnitude has a multi-faceted sense, one has to look closely at the application of this universal and meaningful economic tool in theory and practice.

An important issue in assessing natural resources is the correct application of discounting procedures. The starting point in our deliberations is that the discount rate is part of the price system. Time preferences reflect the fact that people generally use discount rates when estimating future events. The events of the future are given less attention today than the events of the present. The interest rate on borrowed money (financial capital) is a certain level of the minimum discount rate. As there is a risk of various changes in the market of fuel suppliers due to supply disruptions, or even due to the exhaustion of energy resources, it is natural to charge higher discount rates.

Discounting plays a key role in economic policy as well. As a result, there has been a long-running debate, going as far back as the 1930s, over deciding which discount rate to choose.

Concerning the need to discount the depletion and future environmental degradation of non-renewable energy and other resources, the idea of applying a discount rate lower than the market's rate has been circulating since the 1930s. For example, O. Tahvonen and J. Kuuluvainen (1993) have clearly demonstrated that non-polluting technologies can only be competitive with conventional ones, leading to a rise in pollution, if relatively low discount rates are applied. Other scientists believe and argue that applying a discount rate above 5% reflects unsustainable alternatives.

In other words, a much lower, in comparison to the market's, or even zero discount rate is being advocated when considering the need to ensure economic justice for future generations.

In economic models, a juggling between various discount rates is widespread, and most often the only comment or conclusion is that, at a certain discount rate, particular results will be obtained.

To sum up the various views, it can be stated that the discount rate is usually chosen by the commercial sector, taking into account certain considerations. The lowest rate is believed to be the interest rate, i.e. a so-called risk-free investment, but it varies depending on the period. In a good case scenario, it can be around 4%, and in times of crisis, it can reach 9% or more. Adding the influence of risk factors and the percentage of inflation, it is rare to expect a discount rate below 7% in calculations.

However, it should be noted that although the rate at which non-renewable resources are exhausted depends on the discount rate chosen, this dependence is far from unambiguous. In the majority of theoretical models, a higher discount rate results in faster resource depletion. This basic hypothesis can be attributed to the ideas raised by Hotteling (1931). Similar conclusions on the relationship between the discount rate and the quality of the environment in a broader social context were provided by J. A. Krautkramer (1988). He demonstrated that low discount rates underpin environmental protection, but at the same time, encourage the accumulation of productive capital, which indirectly increases the need for natural resources. The formation of this concept is also influenced by D. Lee and D. Orr (1975), who investigated the effect of a private discount rate for the optimal exploitation of non-renewable energy resources in the case of a monopoly.

There is a special phenomenon in regard to RES: the promotion of their use is undoubtedly one of the most important tasks of economic policy. For example, the use of inexhaustible and never-ending sources of solar energy would be an ideal solution for all of society and, therefore, the social discount rate could be considered as zero. However, the bank lends interest to the investor at an interest rate that could be considered as the minimum discount rate. This problem can be solved by covering part of the investment using Structural Funds.

> "There are no simple rules for setting a socially optimal discount rate. Indeed, the choice of a discount rate in such an analysis remains one of the most difficult issues in economic theory because it raises questions that lie beyond this scientific discipline" (Pearce, Markandya and Barbier 1989).

It is, therefore, necessary to find other ways to resolve the conflict between the distribution of wealth between different generations of people. Beckerman has shown that time distributions can be made (at least theoretically) by appropriately selecting the discount level (Beckerman 1994). If natural and man-made capital are substitutes, then the problem of discounting is solved by applying the criterion of non-depleting capital reserves.

Proper evaluation of capital is crucial to the concept of sustainability. J. Pezzey (1992) expressed the view that in order to ensure sustainable economic development, it is necessary to maintain a constant reserve of natural capital or, more precisely, to guarantee a negative change in the reserves of natural resources. As the population continues to grow, existing capital reserves should be increased in order to maintain wealth/wealth reserves per capita. R. M. Solow (1974) proposed an aggregate indicator of changes in capital stocks as a way of measuring sustainable development. He saw the problem of intergenerational equality as the need to guarantee that the fixed capital stock (natural or man-made) that generates total income is sufficient to ensure consumption levels for future generations no smaller than those enjoyed by the present generation. The same goes for Mr Hicks's definition of sustainable income.

Economic policies that are managed in this way, while primarily designed to meet human needs, are also likely to guarantee the survival of nature and its natural population. Only then will sufficient environmental guarantees be possible.

But the key issue is to monetise scarce natural resources and environmental services. Such a theoretical possibility, if it were to be realised in practice, would allow the monetary valuation of natural resources to be included directly into the UN Standardised System of National Accounts created in 1968 (Agenda-21). However, this is, in my opinion, a fundamental mistake. Things valued by money can only be those items that are created by man.

The ability to monetise the effects of the emissions is a key part of the economic approach to the environment. According to R. Čiegis (2002), the socially "correct" (optimal) evaluation of the quantity and quality of different environmental goods means the establishment of a threshold value for environmental goods. The broadening of the boundaries of assets in national accounts, from "fixed" capital to non-produced natural assets such as soil, minerals and forests, and the capacity of the natural environment to absorb air, water and land, provide a broader concept of economic sustainability. However, it is still a compromise.

In 1946, Mr Hicks was the first to develop the fundamental concept of balanced income, which limits income to the maximum sustainable consumption of all types of capital. "Income is the amount that anyone (individual, company, country) can consume without reducing their future consumption potential" (Hicks 1988). According to Hicks, income is the maximum sustainable consumption. If capital is depreciated in the production process, and all other conditions remain unchanged, production opportunities and consumption will inevitably decline in the future. The most important conclusion of Hicks's definition of income is that the stocks (capital) necessary to generate the flow of consumable goods and services must be kept intact. However, his theory is limited to man-made capital.

"The unwillingness to apply this concept to the environment, to natural resources, limiting everything into only man-made capital, has seriously undermined the assessment of economic well-being" (Čiegis 2004).

Meyers has explored productive functions that show the benefits of expanding and investing in knowledge capital (Meyers 1993). A. Marshall stated that "while nature is subject to diminishing returns, human knowledge is subject to increasing returns. Knowledge is the most powerful engine of production" (Marshall 1961). We must agree with Clark's idea that "knowledge is the only instrument of our production that is not subject to diminishing returns" (Clark 1973). "At the end of the Twentieth Century, this approach was recognized again in a new theory of growth treating knowledge as the goods of non-competitive property" (Romer 1986).

The key question is, how are the types of capital used compensated so that sources of economic prosperity are not wasted when consumed in the production process?

Energy is such a special sector of the economy that there is potential for the use of RES, but given their specific characteristics, we need to interpret them from an economic point of view. With regard to our country, it should be noted that there are imports of energy resources—natural gas, oil and coal. Secondary energy—electricity or petroleum products—can also be imported. Thus, the problem of offsetting the used economic factor—the import of energy sources—is a question of ensuring the security of the energy supply. Economic theories now emphasise the importance of renewables as a major substitute for fossil fuels, as well as knowledge capital as the most agile type of capital that has no growth margins, compensating for the exhaustive forms of assets.

However, these efforts require extraordinarily high levels of investment. Given that major energy projects, such as electricity interconnections, are ongoing in the current period, it is also necessary to link liabilities to financing opportunities and economic-financial mechanisms for raising capital. On the other hand, it is clear that if there is a need to base the extent of the implementation of RES on the directives, it implies that the market mechanism is not properly functioning for some reason. It is our job to investigate these causes. In addition, RES development cannot be viewed in isolation from the tendencies of economic developments. The EU directive obligations must be translated into a positive effect, which is the basis for motivating RES programmes in many countries. It is, therefore, necessary to examine the positive macroeconomic effects and various assumptions which make it possible to assess them, and link them to the support measures used.

CHAPTER FOUR

THE VALUE-ADDED ACCOUNTING PROBLEM AND SOLUTION FORMULATION

General principles

Essential aspects of the living or working environment are related to the physical, ecological and social context of the environment as a whole. Natural values have gradually lost their spirit. They have become a natural commodity, as natural resources have become the driving force of the economy. Incorrect attitudes towards the environment and the natural resources that surround us have been the cause of all the problems we are experiencing today. Nature and the whole living environment give us access to the wealth and resources they provide but they cannot supply them to us. All methods of human economic activity are related to the environment around us. Economic development requires natural resources, and, therefore, economic growth depends on natural (environmental) capital or the supply of natural resources. As the economy develops faster, natural resources become scarcer. One of the top priorities of humanity today is to stop further depletion of natural resources. This is not easy due to various reasons such as incompatibilities between different groups, religious and cultural differences, inequalities in the economic development of society and states, differences in the natural environment, and other factors. But one thing we can do is count how much and what exactly we (humans) still have (on earth). It is necessary to carry out an analysis of the natural and created currently owned economic and social capital, to calculate the amount of capital available and to assess its quality. However, the application of such accounting methods requires a different view of sustainable development. From an economic point of view, this assessment depends on the way natural resources are viewed.

The key issue, that makes economic science fundamental and exclusive, is adding value to the production (and service) process.

Added value is created when the income (benefit) exceeds the cost. For an entrepreneur, it is the profit generated by combining various limited production factors—land, labour, capital, raw materials, and energy—in the production or service process. However, certain aspects, such as the negative side effects of production on the environment and human health, remain outside the real estimation. Even where such assessments are made, the estimation is complex and, unfortunately, often ambiguous.

The concept of sustainable development came about when there was an obvious danger to nature that could no longer be denied, which was caused by waste from the production and consumption process. Nowadays, there is widespread talk about the structure of knowledge as a production factor that has obvious value and added value, but has no market price, as it is essentially considered a public good. It is nurtured by the public science and education system, but in the open market, the price of science is still only indirectly measured, such as the brain drain (Schumpeter 2014).

The Sustainable Value-Oriented Methodology for Assessing the Sustainable Performance of Companies and Other Economic Entities has been proposed by English scientists, Figge et al. (2002). The authors suggest a new point of view, called sustainable added value (SAV). The value is created when the benefit exceeds the expenditure, taking into consideration the external costs caused by environmental and social harm. The measure of SAV is exactly the kind of measure which shows how much more value is created by a company being more efficient than the benchmark, and by allocating resources to such a company instead of the benchmark companies. As a result, sustainable eco-social efficiency and the absolute level of use of environmental and social resources are taken into account, so that SAV simultaneously encompasses economic, environmental and social aspects.

From a theoretical point of view, this approach can measure the overall contribution to sustainable development as it thoroughly “translates” the requirements of the Stable Capital Rule at the macro level into measures at the micro-level. However, there are many disadvantages and problems. A company’s added value is defined as the residual value that remains after deduction of the cost of goods and services purchased by the company. SAVs must reflect the total flows of all energy and materials, depending on their relative environmental hazards. This aggregation is achieved by classifying each emission according to its contribution to different environmental issues, which are then classified according to their respective harmfulness. Ecological efficiency is a new way of evaluating the overall contribution to sustainability and can be used in practice because it is based on information available in the UK market, therefore, it is not something absolutely exclusive.

If there is a need to evaluate the ecological, social efficiency and economic activity of a company, there is no need to define the external factors for environmental and social effect in material expression.

SAV combines the productivity and efficiency of all three dimensions of sustainability. As SAV provides clear information about the amount of generated value and ensures constant environmental and social activity, it is, therefore, based on the paradigm of ecology. In material terms, SAV shows the additional generated value of the company, assimilated with all changes of ecological and social efficiency.

On a national scale, GDP is considered to be the indicator of added value. It consists of the labour costs, used capital in terms of amortisation, taxes and profits. The growth of GDP is considered to be the main indicator of the country's advancement.

The need to evaluate advancement not only in terms of growth but also in other aspects of sustainable development encourages scientists and practitioners responsible for the direct implementation of economic policy to look for solutions. The potential solution lies in the correct evaluation of the result of economic activity. One of the directions in terms of the synthesis of the research and practical activity is the theoretical and practical reasoning of sustainable development indicators, evaluating the result of economic activity, e.g. dynamics of the Real Advancement Indicator calculated in the United States (Norgaard, 2001). Incorporating certain scientifically reasoned adjustments to the GDP calculations, the indicator has shown a downturn tendency since 1965. Currently, the indicator is even lower than 45 years ago. One of the main adjustments is the interpretation of the environmental restoration costs as negative in the calculation of the Real Advancement Indicator, instead of positive, as in the case of calculating GDP.

In principle, this approach may also be applicable in the field of energetics when assessing the sustainability aspects of the use of different types of energy, but more research is needed to confirm such a concept. The research will require two directions: first, empirical research is needed to examine both the practicality of the method and the results that can be achieved in actual countries, starting with Lithuania. Second, future research should examine the institutional and organisational conditions and the readiness of trading or market schemes to evaluate SAV. This contribution can be expressed in economic, environmental or social terms. In economic terms, SAV expresses in absolute monetary terms the sustainability of a company or country as a whole.

The necessity and principles of green accounting in order to redesign energy development planning in accordance with the principles of sustainability

The need for green accounting can be justified in order to demonstrate the ecological impact of individual fuels and energy uses on climate change indicators.

Table 3-1. GHG emission factors in energy industries
Source: Lithuanian national inventory report 2019: Greenhouse gas emissions 1990-2017.

Energy industries	Emission factors in the study of 2018, t/TJ		
	CO_2	CH_4	N_2O
Liquid fuel			
Motor gasoline	72.77	0.003	0.0006
Diesel	72.73	0.003	0.0006
Gasoil	72.73	0.003	0.0006
Residual fuel oil	78.4	0.003	0.0006
Petroleum coke	94.06	0.003	0.0006
Non-liquified petroleum gas	56.9	0.001	0.0001
Orimulsion	81.74	0.003	0.0006
Shale oil	76.6	0.003	0.0006
Liquified petroleum	66.34	0.001	0.0001
Crude oil	77.74	0.003	0.0006
Solid fuel			
Other bituminous coal	95.1	0.001	0.0015
Anthracite	106.55	0.001	0.0015
Sub-bituminous coal	96.1	0.001	0.0015
Peat	104.34	0.001	0.0015
Natural gas			
Natural gas	55.14*	0.001	0.0001
Biomass			
Wood and wood waste	101.34	0.03	0.004
Other type of solid biomass	103.69	0.03	0.004
Biogas	58.45	0.001	0.0001
Waste			

Municipality waste (RES)	109.03	0.03	0.004
Municipality waste (non-RES)	111.65	0.03	0.004
Industrial waste	143	0.03	0.004

Environmental accounting or "green" accounting models are increasingly being used alongside basic economic accounting systems and tools in the EU and worldwide. "Green" environmental accounting models take into account the hidden costs of economic activity; therefore, the "green" accounting system is superior in terms of environmental and sustainable development. Even though energy economics in Lithuania are managed according to the principles of the sustainable economic management system, priority is given to the cost of the direct production method. In developing or "transitional" economies, priority is given to the scenario of economic growth. Natural resources are being managed and environmental concerns addressed through short-term goals, with aspects and indicators of sustainable development used solely to enhance the reports, leaving the burden of responsibility of decision-making to future generations.

The assessment of the sustainable development of the energy sector may be based on environmental accounting, green accounting or environmental accounting models. One of the proponents of alternative economic theory, H. Daly, sees growth as the quantitative development of the economy, either physically or monetarily. The economy is not isolated from the environment in which we live, so as our knowledge grows, the economy grows and we realise that potential changes in the structure of physical stocks are taking place. H. Daly explains that quantitative economic development in high-income countries is irrational because it reduces economic efficiency and serves only to meet current needs. Furthermore, it increases the threat to economic security and worsens the ecological status. In the light of H. Daly's ideas on economic development, he concludes that economic activity must be wise in relation to the ecological capacity of ecosystems. Classical macroeconomic theories favour a steady growth economy where Daly's proposals to limit or reduce consumption are unacceptable. A growing economy promotes long-term wage growth, which is linked to the creation of jobs. H. Daly's statements encourage the search for alternative ways of development so that development is sustainable and does not adversely affect the environment. In classical economic theory, economic growth is associated with the growth of the gross national product. However, there is the natural capital aspect, which is being rapidly consumed as the economy grows, therefore, it decreases. Gross National Product (GNP) and GDP do not estimate the depreciation of natural capital and the costs and damage caused by pollution. GNP and GDP are measures of consumption, production and income, rather than wealth. Such a disadvantage exists in the whole system of national accounts, which does not include the value of natural and environmental resources in the calculation of indicators because natural capital is considered free of charge. National accounts only measure current indicators and, therefore, do not assess the long-term effects of development and do not reflect, and even underestimate, the depreciation of natural capital and environmental damage. However, sustainable development can be achieved by replacing quantitative growth with qualitative economic development, i.e. when development takes place without growth. In order for sustainable economic development to bring benefit rather than harm, we need to move away from the accelerating growth that is now increasingly affecting the environment and society on a large scale (Daly and Cobb 1994).

The capital-driven economy is shifting much of its production to China, but continues to promote a consumerist culture, increases emigration numbers and promotes social inequality. Although the main economic indicators (GDP, GNP) are increasing, the real living environment is deteriorating due to the unevaluated hidden costs and ecological aspects. In real terms, economic progress would be much lower than currently calculated and expressed in GNP (Čiegis 2004). When calculating GDP or GNP, all effects of economic development should be taken into account; thus, it is necessary to calculate and systematise all indicators of sustainable development. A thorough evaluation of the indicators helps to assess both the positive and negative effects of the activity.

Sustainable development indicators are usually designed to describe specific activities of the sector (economic, environmental, social). As the concept of sustainable development has been developed for the analysis of the activities of the economic sector and for solving environmental impact issues, most of the indicators are related to the economic and environmental sectors.

A comprehensive understanding of sustainable development methodologies and the successful application of sustainable development indicators in practice are not easy tasks. The concept of sustainable development is relatively new, and the uncertainty and abundance of criteria are misleading or rather frightening for consumers and producers, so their practical application is not a mass phenomenon. The idea of sustainable development was formed several decades ago, and the concept itself was formulated only in 1992—only at the end of the previous century, therefore, researchers are continuing to improve the methodology of sustainable development, looking for ways to adapt the sustainable development criteria in practice, and for analysis and evaluation of each activity in regards to these criteria. What is more, scientists are looking for and analysing the positive and negative reasons for implementing sustainable development, using various measures and indicators. These indicators, depending on their structure, can be distributed into two groups: simple and complex. Simple indicators are used to define one particular activity of a sector (e.g. GDP per capita, greenhouse gas emissions, concentration levels of pollution in cities, etc.). The EU Sustainable Development Strategy has a list of 155 indicators divided into 10 groups according to their type. As mentioned earlier, in the National Strategy of Sustainable Development of Lithuania, approximately 100 indicators are listed. Even though, in general, the number of indicators is quite extensive, they are relatively easy to calculate and analyse, therefore, they are quite often found in reports, and are provided in national and EU statistical databases. Also, such indicators are much more useful in the decision-making process, therefore, are often used as an instrument for making certain important decisions. The Lisbon Strategy provides 14 structural indicators, where the indicator for greenhouse gas emissions is ascribed to the group of environmental indicators. Other indicators are mostly used to characterise economic activities.

One single indicator, which could cover all areas of sustainable development, is rarely used in practice and in decision-making due to its complexity and highly inconvenient structure. Most often, complex indicators are used to describe sustainable development, analysing all three sectors (economic, natural and social environment). According to the list of indicators provided in the National Strategy for Sustainable Development, it is possible to separately calculate the indicators of economic, social or ecological sustainable development, which can be obtained by averaging the indicators of one sector. The overall sustainable development indicator is calculated by averaging the values of the sectorial sustainability indicators (Čiegis 2009). However, in practice, it is much more common to use complex indicators for measuring only two sectors, i.e. economic and natural environment, or economic and social environment.

For simplicity and ease of calculation, the most commonly used are the indicators of the carbon footprint (CO_2) and energy efficiency. The following indicators help to evaluate the natural economic environment and the natural environment: ecological footprint, environmental space index, material intensity per service unit (MIPS), green national product, environmental protection, environmental sustainability index, and ecological rucksack. The following indicators are relevant to the economic and social environment: Human Development Index, a measure of economic welfare, and the Economic Aspects of Welfare Index, net domestic product (GNP), sustainable economic welfare index, real progress indicator, sustainable process index, and others.

Reports published by the World Wildlife Fund (WWF) provide interesting facts about the sustainable development sector. The Living Planet Report, published by WWF in 2012, provides a different approach to assessing sustainability criteria when measuring economic activity using the ecological footprint method.

Today, different aspects of sustainable development are being addressed. Various scientists explain that sustainable development is theoretically and methodologically viewed as uncertain—the main problem is that human presence on earth becomes incompatible with the surrounding environment (nature and society). A different approach to sustainable development—growth without growth or the intangible concept of development based on the social principles of development—has been explored in published scientific papers by J. Rifkin (2012), T. Jackson (2009), M. Wackernagel (1999), D. D. Moran (2008), W. E. Rees (2000), J. Kitzes (2010), and K. H. Robe (2002).

The Ecological Footprint as an accounting tool for economic sustainability

The Ecological Footprint (EF) is a measure indicating how many biosphere resources—fertile land and marine areas—are needed to meet human consumption needs and absorb the waste they leave. In 2003, the world's EF was 14.1 billion global hectares—2.2 global hectares per person (global hectare is a measure defining average global needs). However, the total area of productive land in 2003 was only 11.2 billion global hectares or 1.8 global hectares per person. Humanity consumes more than the planet can create.

The EF is the productive area of land needed to meet our annual human consumption, providing energy and natural resources and absorbing pollution from human activities. A country is considered to develop in an environmentally sustainable manner, and the resilience and functionality of ecosystems are considered to be intact provided that this "consumed" area of land does not exceed the maximum productive area and its biological capacity.

In addition, the EF is the amount of bio-productive land required to meet annual consumption, i.e. provide resources, energy, and assimilate the pollution of that year caused by technology and resource management. The bio-productivity and regenerative capacity of the territory being analysed will not be impaired if the total EF of the population does not exceed the maximum bio-productive area. In such a case, it can be stated that the development of the territory does not harm ecological sustainability.

The EF consists of five types of area, reflecting the consumption of renewable resources: pasture area, crop area, a fertile area with buildings and roads, water area for fish stocks, and forest area for timber. The consumption of secondary products, such as meat, milk and paper, is also included in the EF, after converting it to the number of primary products (cattle, wood and water) used in their production. Non-renewable resources are included in the European Parliament (EP) only on the basis of their impact on nature's regenerative capacity. More precisely, the forest area, which is necessary to assimilate the pollution generated by the use of fossil fuels, is calculated. It should be noted that the productivity of different territories is not the same, so in order to be able to compare, each hectare is translated into a "global hectare" (gha), the productivity of which is equivalent to the world average of that year. This way, the hectare of more than average land is equivalent to more than one "global hectare". If the calculated EF estimate (gha) exceeds the country's maximum bio-productive area (gha), then it is concluded that the country has an ecological deficit. From one perspective, the ecological deficit can be covered by imports of natural resources from other countries. On the other hand, if a country does not import natural resources, it means that the flow of natural resources consumed by its population exceeds the rate of natural regeneration, and, as a result, the country's reserves of natural resources are reduced. In this case, this would imply that the country under analysis could be characterised as ecologically unsustainable (Rees, 2000).

Using the EF Indicator, we can figure out the current demand for resources and gather information about the presence of resources, but we cannot predict the tendencies of resource fluctuation. We can find out how many hectares of forest are needed to absorb the particular amount of CO_2. It is estimated that one global hectare (gha) of forest per year can absorb as much CO_2 as is emitted after burning 1,450 litres of gasoline.

According to Wackernagel and Rees (1998), three methods are used to calculate the EF. The first method of calculating the EF is based on the calculation of the amount of land needed to produce a certain amount of energy in agriculture and forestry. Calculation results are expressed in hectares (ha). Replacement products include ethanol obtained from agricultural production and methanol from the forestry industry.

The second method suggests estimating the amount of forest area required to absorb a certain amount of pollutant emissions from burning fossil fuels. This approach was widely used in EF assessment reports by

Bicknell et al. (1998); Ferng (2002); Haberl et al. (2001); Van den Bergh and Grazi (2010); and Wackernagel et al. (1999).

The third method suggests calculating the value of alternative energy sources by evaluating the amount of land they occupy, and the amount of land needed to build and equip them, which would ensure the same energy demand as the fossil fuel. For example, a forest with a corresponding energy value must compensate for the amount of energy used to replant the forest area by burning fossil fuels.

The Living Planet Index

The Living Planet Index, published by the WWF (2010), shows the change in biodiversity and estimates the change (expressed in percentage or units) of endangered and rare plant and animal species. The index shows the effects of human activities and their impact on ecosystems. This index can help identify the locations, areas and measures needed to restore sensitive and endangered ecosystems.

Ecosystem services are the benefits of ecosystems provided to humans, which can be categorised as follows:

- Direct supply services are services or products obtained directly from nature (food, wood, medicinal plants, biofuels, etc.).
- Regulated services are obtained by regulating natural processes occurring in nature (water and wastewater cleaning and processing, climate control, pollination of plants).
- Supporting services control the key ecological functions and processes required for the ecosystem processes to successfully function (nutrient metabolism, photosynthesis, soil formation, composting).
- Cultural services refer to the psychological and emotional benefits provided by nature and the ecosystem (fostering a recreational environment, aesthetic and spiritual experiences).

The total EF is the sum of the individual ecological footprints combined. The following components of the EF are distinguished: carbon dioxide, pastures, forests, fishing grounds, crops, and built-up areas.

The CO_2 footprint, or carbon uptake index, is the amount of forest area required to absorb CO_2 emissions from fuel combustion, land consolidation and chemical processes.

The pasture footprint is an index showing the amount of land needed to supply meat, dairy, fur, leather and wool products.

The forest footprint is the indicator showing the amount of forest product (timber, paper, biofuels, firewood) consumption per capita.

The fishing footprint is an index showing the yield of primary produce—fish and other marine products. The index evaluates data for 1439 marine and 268 freshwater species.

The crop footprint is the index showing the amount of land needed to grow food, feed, oilseeds, and rubber products.

The build-up footprint is the index showing the amount of land that is covered by houses, roads, factories, hydroelectric and other types of power plants, reservoirs and other man-made buildings and structures.

Footprints of CO_2, built-up areas and forests play the key role in energetics.

To find out whether our presence on earth is not a burden for the ecosystem, we first need to determine the resilience of the ecosystems as regards human impact and activity. Therefore, the so-called biocapacity needs to be calculated.

The importance of EF has increased significantly in recent years. This is mainly due to human activities which create extremely high levels of CO_2 emissions.

The modified EF is calculated by multiplying the final energy consumption, using different energy sources, taking into account the land use index, and adding the result to the total EF of the energy supply cycle. The following indicators, taking into account the cost of energy transportation, are used to calculate the size of the ecological footprint: the available data on energy production, storage, transportation, transmission and security aspects. These allow the annual consumption (kg) of the highest input (i) to be studied. The majority of the data comes from statistical tables, but business plans or company reports can be used as well.

Part IV

The Prerequisites for the Sustainable Growth of Renewable Energy based on Spatial Energy Planning

CHAPTER ONE

THE SYMBIOSIS OF NATIONAL GOAL IMPLEMENTATION PROGRAMMES

The National Energy Independency Strategy, approved in 2018, states that in 2020, the energy made in Lithuania should account for 35% of the total consumed energy, in 2030 for 70%, and in 2050 for 100%. Also, the strategy declares that in 2020, the energy generated from RES will account for 30% of the total final energy consumed in the country, in 2030 for 45%, and in 2050 for 80%. Energy generated from RES will become the main source of energy in all sectors—electricity, heating, cooling and transport. The strategy also states that Lithuania has to make an important transition from an energy technology importing country to an energy technology generating and exporting country.

In order to find solutions to a wide variety of issues, it is essential to create clear guidelines and directions. As experience shows, the most harmful case scenario would be an undefined national policy and uncoordinated efforts of different policymakers. Basically, the implementation of RES synchronically solves a variety of other problems, the localisation of which from a territorial point of view, is of utmost importance. Professor R. Čiegis has very aptly expressed the basic idea: "If global civilization hopes to solve the global ecological crisis, it requires decentralized, flexible, community-based responsibility" (Čiegis, 1997).

It is necessary to identify the local demand and supply potential for RES in cities, as well as the long-term vision and its implementation process, especially the financing sources. This is what is lacking in the majority of cases. Even though cities receive quite a lot of investments into RES technologies, usually it is based on individual, chaotic projects, which do not belong to a long-term, thorough, well-thought-out strategy. Investors themselves decide which technologies and solutions are trending at that moment, or what are the most convenient to finance, e.g. mass transfer of the heating sector to the use of biofuels, instead of selecting the most appropriate options for certain territories. What is more, the decision-makers in local authorities often lack the knowledge and resources to evaluate the territorial potential of different types of RES and plan the most efficient implementation.

Considering the fact that approximately 75% of the European population lives in cities, according to the statistical data of Eurostat, EU city territories are some of the most difficult areas in terms of EU energy consumption and greenhouse gas emission sources, which have a major effect on climate change. At the same time, cities are the main drivers of EU economics, creating new jobs and perfect conditions for economic growth. Currently, lots of attention is being given to the development of the new EU Climate Strategy, according to the obligations of the Paris Agreement. The key accent of this strategy is the mass use of RES. The majority of European cities are currently preparing their individual long-term strategies up to 2050. Lots of cities already have actual plans prepared regarding how to make sure that 100% of the energy demand is satisfied using only RES.

It is necessary to enable the assessment of external benefit for the use of RES, which is usually not assessed for individual projects. Support measures for the use of RES often contradict the market patterns due to short-term goals, which is one of the main disadvantages in nearly all countries. These measures do not shape uniform technological programmes over long-term periods. The sustainable growth of renewable energy is based on the formulated methodology, which enables us to achieve maximum benefit with minimal support for beneficiaries as well as for the state. Results after evaluations of external benefits for solar, wind, and geothermal energy projects in urban areas could be interpolated and used for the assessment of selected technology or a support scheme for wider use in the context of spatial energy planning.

Summarising what has been said in the preceding chapters, we must once again state that harmonious progress is a form of economic and social evolution that meets the needs of the present without compromising future generations. When talking about future generations, it is not just human beings, but all kinds of life relying on land, water, and natural resources for their existence. The forest acts as a defensive bastion, transforming the exhaled and produced CO_2 into fresh air. Recognising the laws of Nature's evolution, while also realising the duty to Nature's revitalisation, is called harmonious progress. It refers to the aspirations of restoring a covenant with Nature, which is already—in a form of episodically conscious human action—being realised and rationalised in the dynamics of time. This is not just about replacing burning fuels with RES. It is a whole set of measures and assumptions, including the preservation of forests and increasing forest areas as much as possible. And yet, it's just a part of the tremendous work and huge change that the new paradigm demands.

These philosophical ideas perfectly connect with those of the most famous economists of the time, R. Constanza and H. Daly. I present a large excerpt from their article, as it reflects the need to reform the postulates of economic theory in order to be consistent with the new paradigm of interaction between nature and man.

> A minimum necessary condition for sustainability is the maintenance of the total natural capital stock at or above the current level. This constancy of natural capital rule can thus be seen as a prudent minimum condition for assuring sustainability. We differentiate the concepts of growth (material increase in size) and development (improvement in the organization without size change). Given these definitions, growth cannot be sustainable indefinitely on a finite planet. One problem is that current measures of economic well-being at the macro level (i.e. the Gross National Product) measure mainly growth. This urgently requires revision. Finally, we suggest some principles of sustainable development and describe why maintaining natural capital stocks is a prudent and achievable policy for ensuring sustainable development (Constanza and Daly 1992).

We can build on the tendencies and breakthroughs that have emerged during this period, which are precisely the steps towards a state in which the meaning of man and human life in relation to Nature can be expected. This is the concept of the circular economy and the first practical tests. The theoretical concept of the Happiness Economy, the Green Settlement Movement, smart cities, smart networks, and urban initiatives to reach 100 per cent provision of RES over a period of time—all of this is encouraging but dominated by the predatory exploitation of Nature under the guise of a beautiful welfare economy concept.

Before analysing the challenges posed by the evolution of the harmonious progress of energy in relation to economic theory, one has to mention the most important/crucial moment—the financing problem, which is the main obstacle in the current economic paradigm. A recent study by Constanza et al. (2017) estimates that the global cost of implementing the Paris Agreement would be trillions of dollars under various scenarios. These are the findings of a highly authoritative team of eminent authors. However, in my opinion, the cost alone is not enough. In essence, the problem is the distribution of wealth between different generations. This is precisely the most important obstacle, causing resistance or delaying of decisions by governments. However, this is the result of ignorance and also resistance from fossil and biofuel lobbyists. Support for the deployment of RES technologies is justified economically as well as by the enormous synergistic effect of the deployment of natural RES technologies in the current investment period. There is, therefore, a need for a sound justification for the use of financial resources for harmonious energy progress, demonstrating that there is no conflict between sustainable development, focused on the very long term, and the maximisation of wealth during this period. It refers to the distribution of wealth between different generations of people. Without state support for this process, the application of RES technologies will be stalled or become one-sided. However, clarification is needed as to the basis and substance of state support at this critical moment.

The harmonious progress of energy can and must be interpreted in the context of all human economic activity, which implies much broader challenges that may be solved by certain shifts in the development of economic theory. Economic theory goes beyond what seems to be above its reach and the idea of welfare economics evolves into the aspirations of an economy of happiness. In other words, advancement is no longer viewed only as economic growth, and the pursuit of human well-being and happiness is no longer seen only as an increase in income. In essence, it is the merit of the knowledge economy, combining the knowledge of economics and psychology. An extremely progressive idea of the circular economy is beginning to emerge in connection with Nature. However, there is a need for a broader and more comprehensive assessment of the potential of the circular economy to establish itself in a life where competition is still dominant, a prerogative of growth over quality. Energetics can be a flagship on this path, but there are still obstacles to be overcome and the organisational preconditions for this process to be discussed. Figure 4-1 depicts the main directions of national goal implementation programmes.

Only by consolidating resources in a unified direction can we solve financial problems, which at the moment appear to be quite dangerous. For example, Germany has set ambitious policies for increasing renewable energy shares and decommissioning nuclear energy, but there are certain scientific gaps in how this transition should occur, especially when considering all energy sectors. There is a study aimed at advancing the knowledge of transitioning the German energy system to 100 per cent renewable energy by 2050.

> Taking into consideration renewable resource potentials, energy system costs and primary energy supply, this study develops a path for transitioning the German energy system within the heating, industrial, transport and electricity sectors. The analysis demonstrates that it is possible to carry out this transition from a technical and economic perspective with some measures being vital for achieving this ambition in a cost-effective manner. The most significant challenge in this transition is regarding resource potentials where especially biomass resources are constrained and under

pressure. Finally, the most influential measures for achieving the renewable transition are discussed (Hansen, Mathiesen and Skov 2019).

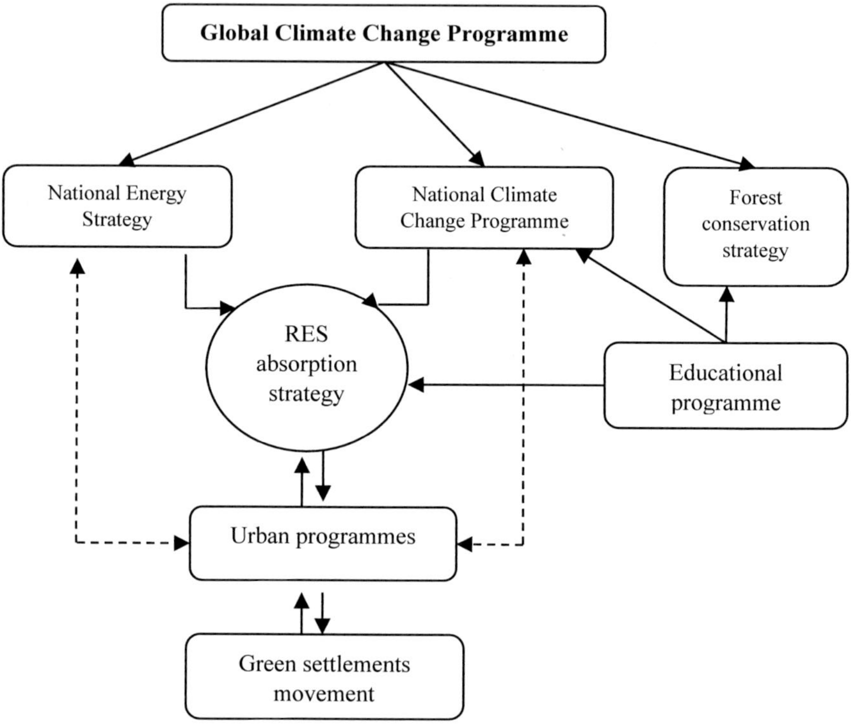

Fig. 4-1. The symbiosis of national goal implementation programmes

In the following sections, we will discuss the path for applying the knowledge in order to achieve the goals of human-Nature harmony that have already been discussed. The main practical solution could be establishing clear links between the goals that the state then defines in different individual programmes.

CHAPTER TWO

THE ROLE OF CITIES IN RES TECHNOLOGY IMPLEMENTATION

The problem of assessing the impact of certain types of energy from RES

There is no consensus among scientists in the debate on who should take the initiative and have responsibility for addressing the issues of the dissemination of innovation as a precondition for economic development: the state, the city or private structures. The basic idea of the above problem has been expressed by a prominent environmentalist: "Global thinking must move towards a local one because localities exist within the boundaries of nature, where global exists only in the offices of the World Bank and the ICF and in multinational offices. Global ecological space is the local integration of everything" (Shiva 1992). More and more scientists say that decisions are needed in this area by territorial units.

According to the "Summary for Urban Policy Makers", launched by the Intergovernmental Panel on Climate Change (IPCC), climate science must be accessible to urban policymakers. Otherwise, there will be no chance of limiting global warming to 1.5°C. The main goal of the Special Report on Global Warming of 1.5°C (SR1.5), written by 18 authors, was to produce the Summary for Urban Policymakers to translate the report's key scientific findings and policy observations for officials and policymakers of the world's cities and urban areas.

> In cities and urban areas, there are actions that policymakers—along with residents and stakeholders, such as civil society, the academic community, and those in business and finance—can take to help limit warming and adapt to the impacts of climate change. The effects of a city's actions are not limited to its own borders or region, and, likewise, lessons learned in some cities and urban areas can serve as inspiration and resources for solutions in other urban areas (Bazas et al. 2018).

Even though in the context of today's events these thoughts and guidelines seem quite utopic, I believe none of you would have chosen to read this book if there wasn't a possibility of reacting to the situation and starting to move in the right direction. My goal is not to frighten you about the potentially upcoming Apocalypse, on the contrary, I believe there is still hope for humanity. Faith gives me optimism, which is the basis of any positive action. As stated by the famous natural scientist, humble ideas, even though exceptionally good in theory, eventually end up in the drawers of officials, and only the urban policymakers have the power to put them into action (Fromm, 2008).

"The SR1.5 identifies cities and urban areas as one of four critical global systems that can accelerate and upscale climate action but recognizes this will require major transitions in how both mitigation and adaptation are undertaken" (Bazas et al. 2018). The Summary for Urban Policymakers strives to initiate the discussion with city practitioners and policymakers, as well as leading city networks and non-governmental organisations. It seeks to provide urban stakeholders access to the most advanced science on why the transition to a 1.5°C world is necessary and how it can be achieved.

In addition to the optimistic view, based on thousands of good practice examples, I provide directions, based on many years of scientific and practical experience. Also, next to energetics, I allow myself to declare unconditional love for nature and trees, both of which are essential for our future. I believe that we have to step back and finally appreciate nature and the natural resources that are still available to us human beings by feeling the pulse of nature and coexisting, rather than interfering with it.

Sources of renewable energy are among the main pillars for the development of sustainable energy, defined as energy production and consumption, ensuring long-term objectives of humanity for each country's development in all social, economic, and environmental aspects. Attention should be focused on the fact that renewability means absolute infinity and inexhaustibility of resources, as well as optimistic statements regarding the potential of energy supply in the future. In economic terms, the phenomenon of RES can be defined as an increase in demand, which envisages massive growth and stimulates cost reduction of technologies, due to the economies of scale and competition.

The use of renewable energy in rural as well as urban areas was a significant development thus adding to the mitigation of climate change, reducing differences between rural and urban-dwelling options, (Harmaajärvi 2000) bringing new RES options for diversifying the energy supply (Palojarvi 2013). The role of local governance for energy and urban development appears highly important here (Tzoulas 2007).

Policies and measures that aim at enhancing the use of RES are mainly driven by EU policy. The scientific problem is the evaluation of the social utility of RES that can show the advantages which are underestimated in investment decisions (Bulkeley and Betsill 2005) and (Kalenda 2007). Moreover, it is a transfer of their economic interpretations on uniform rules and economic laws into a specified dimension, in this case trying to reduce different opinions as much as possible (Bayulken and Huisingh 2015).

However, only certain types of RES, such as solar, thermal (aerothermal, geothermal, hydrothermal), wind, and hydro (incl. waves, tidal, etc.) energy, are inexhaustible. Other resources, such as biomass, depend on economic activity or economic processes, and on the abundance of forests, their proper maintenance, fostering, and use. Industrial and municipal solid waste is another type of biomass assigned to renewables which could be converted to energy, e.g. landfill gas, biogas from farming, and municipal waste in urban areas. These gases could be used via the biodegrading process or via direct burning. The concept of renewability is notional and depends on conditionally constant accumulation. Therefore, the aforementioned sources of biomass could be only relatively viewed as renewables.

Certainly, every type of RES has its advantages and disadvantages. Some types of RES, such as solar or geothermal energy, even though scattered in nature, have a certain specific characteristic: the willingness of consumers to use renewables for energy generation for their own needs and not for sales, and thus joining the energy development process on a wide scale.

In order to make competition opportunities equal for consumers who generate energy from RES for their own needs, and for companies, who generate energy for sale, a specific problem needs to be solved. It is the concept of external public benefit which is difficult to assess and repay for the consumers, as well as implementing the "mission" and using RES technologies at their own risks. There are millions of consumers, thus, knowledge transmission among them is the key factor. There are tremendous possibilities to foster the implementation process of RES technologies (especially solar, wind, and geothermal energy) in this field. However, the development trend of these technologies has been rather poorly investigated, therefore, some countries start subsidising consumers, e.g. a share of the investment is repaid for the installation of solar collectors. Social benefit is usually assigned to the business; however, its main motivator is profit, definitely not the social needs of the population, and certainly not meeting the energy needs of future generations. Consumers can be motivated by indirect subsidising. Therefore, the benefit is understood as the reduced impact on the environment and the solving of certain social problems. However, in practice, the use of RES is still plagued by significant problems.

Recently, various critical remarks concerning the promotion measures for the implementation of RES technologies and energy production from RES have increased. One of the most principal disadvantages of the promotional measures, which worries both the scientific community and practitioners, can be observed in almost all countries: measures for the promotion of RES frequently contradict market rules and distort market signals (Ciarreta, Gutiérrez-Hita and Nasirov 2011), (EURELECTRIC 2004), (European Commission 2014) and (Asmelash 2015). Moreover, they are used to implement short-term objectives and do not create a unified, long-term oriented programme. The newest EU technical document, respecting the formation of support schemes for the promotion of renewable energy technologies, indicates the necessity to revise currently existing RES support measures that provoke market failures.

> With growing renewables shares, poor design and implementation of public intervention has led to unnecessary distortions with regards to energy production, trade and investment in renewables. This raises the cost of promotion of the renewables and risks hampering both the further growth of renewables and the completion of the internal electricity market (European Commission 2013).

An EU document proclaims that support for RES technologies is often unbalanced.

> Renewable energy producers have faced a range of frequent changes to support schemes. Change is constant. In the renewables sector, the regulatory risk that comes with such changes has a direct impact on capital financing costs, the costs of project development and, therefore, with the whole process of developing renewables (European Commission 2013).

Renewable energy policy is a complex system where the balance among three aspects of sustainability—environment, economy, and social life—is needed. A well-performing and balanced RES policy requires efforts from different groups of stakeholders. Even though each country has different starting conditions, namely, developed technical infrastructure and owned energy resources, the development of energy from RES should be shaped on the basis of long-term macroeconomic policy. This means that a good and scientifically based theoretical background is needed, as well as the indicators reflecting economic development and a method for assessing the impact of certain types of energy from RES according to these indicators. The following chapter will deal with the mentioned issues.

The spatial aspect of assessing the benefit of using RES technologies in urban areas

Sustainable energy development is a process of energy production and consumption, ensuring the long-term goals of the state and of mankind, and is consistent with social, economic, and environmental dimensions. In other words, this is a reliable energy supply at an affordable price, causing the lowest possible negative impact on the environment.

RES are more evenly distributed in the world, compared to organic fuel resources, however, a range of factors, such as competing for land use, environmental restrictions in the area, and the operation period for wind and solar energy installations, limit the economic potential of RES. Support for RES is required in order to promote wider use of renewable energy. Energy market failure is a serious obstacle in the promotion of the development of RES. The external positive benefit of using RES as a public good has also not been evaluated. This benefit is related to the introduction of new technologies, their development, and the positive impact on the environment. Subordinating market mechanisms, reducing renewable energy adaptation costs, increasing competitiveness in the market and promoting their development, is required to overcome the aforementioned market failures and other market barriers. What is more, subsidies for RES could be applied or obligatory purchase quotas aimed at energy produced from RES could be introduced.

The market does not ensure the financing of long-term research and development. New energy technologies are permanently impacted by the barriers in all parts of the energy innovation chain (from research and development to dissemination of demonstration projects, information and technologies).

The most important question in our research is the evaluation of the progress of reliability and other sustainable development areas from the territorial aspect. The territorial dimension means the implementation of the management principle while evaluating the sustainability components of energy resources in line with defining the limits of liability.

> Throughout the world, increasing attention is being paid to climate change mitigation. But while ambitious national targets are hard to come by, several regions, cities, towns, institutions, and individuals have taken matters into their own hands. Rather than awaiting international agreement or national targets, these established their own ambitious targets for reducing carbon dioxide emissions and are in the process of finding ways and means to meet these targets. Various levels serve as the impetus for more ambitious targets by demonstrating a will to policymakers as well as finding and demonstrating

> feasible options. It helps confront the previous paradigm that fossil-fuelled economies are the only viable options and renewable energy systems cannot supply the required energy services at a competitive cost (Ostergaard and Lund 2010).

Statistical methods, based on the historical data or selected sectors, could be employed for assessing the development of RES and their impact on the macroeconomic indicators. This general trend could not provide a deep insight into the actual impact on the parameters of a single project. Following general trends can make the benefits of the individual project invisible to the country's macroeconomic indicators. They provide neither the tools nor the techniques to enable the optimisation of RES sector development or the introduction of support measures for maximising the macroeconomic benefits with minimum resources. Therefore, the assessment is inseparable from the microeconomic analysis of the project chosen by the individual investor (taking into account the economic benefits for the developer), using the external parameters which affect the macroeconomic indicators. Results obtained in a single project can be interpolated to assess the potential impact of the support scheme at a national level.

Levelized cost of energy (LCOE) is one of the most popular approaches for comparison of different energy generation options on an equal basis. The present value of the total life cycle cost is calculated considering the chosen discount rate and allocated energy per unit. The LCOE is used to assess the competitiveness of different energy generation options, quantifying the possible gains for the project developer. The elaborated LCOE approach, which was applied in a paper of V. Bobinaite and D. Tarvydas (2014) provides an opportunity to quantitatively assess the influence of certain RES support measures on the cost of energy production. It provides the investor with a tool that can be used to compare different RES investment projects. However, an approach disclosing the principles for assessment of the research methods is required. An external benefit analysis for small wind power plants, geothermal heat pumps, and solar collectors was performed to find their niche in urban and rural areas. The external effect indicators for different case scenarios are shown in Table 4-1.

Table 4-1. The external benefit of using solar, wind and geothermal energy technologies (case of Lithuania)

Indicators	Wind power plants		Geothermal heat pump and solar collectors in a multifamily building	Solar collectors in district heating system
	4 kW	*10kW*	*126kW*	*7000kW*
Production, MWh	6.8	7.5	185	4500
Domestic capital, 1000 EUR	8.02	21.08	25.01	1380.88
Social insurance, 1000 EUR	0.81	1.51	9.27	119.23
Personal income taxes, 1000 EUR	0.29	0.55	3.46	44.46
New jobs (man months)	2.3	4.2	31.9	409.4

Table 4-1 shows the comparison of external benefit using different types and scale of RES. Large-scale solar collectors generate heat mostly during the summer period, whereas wind power plants and the combination of geothermal heat pumps and solar collectors in multi-family buildings provide the effect during the whole year. The main indicators of external benefits are considered to be the use of domestic capital, taxes paid to the state budget, and newly created job places. A combination of different types of RES may create a large external effect and make a significant impact not only on the individual consumers of RES but on society as well. Therefore, the benefit of using RES, especially in urban areas, should be evaluated during the decision-making process.

Currently, the largest share of the global population lives in urban areas, therefore, uniting ecological and urban development problems gained more importance in research during the last decade (Tzoulas et al. 2007) and (Bulkeley and Betsill 2005). The use of renewable energy in rural as well as urban areas became a significant development thus adding to the mitigation of climate change, (de Vries, van Vuuren and Hoogwijk 2007) and (Panwar, Kaushik and Kothari 2011) reducing differences between rural and urban-dwelling options (Bergmann, Colombo and Hanley 2007), bringing new RES options for diversifying the energy supply (Hofierka and Kaňuk 2009) and (Chong et al. 2011). The role of local governance in energy and urban development appears highly important here (Droege 2008) and (Broto and Bulkeley 2012).

Encouraging energy producers and consumers to use RES is one of the major goals of energy policy in Lithuania and other countries. Policies and measures that seek to enhance the use of RES are mainly driven by EU policy. Unstable state energy policy and changes in incentive measures destabilise investment initiatives. The lack of economic evaluation on both the demand and supply sides is the main challenge in achieving the expected goal. An unreasonably huge role is assigned to biomass in the projections of the use of RES. Biomass is an energy resource that is the result of economic activity and depends on the continuity of economic activity. Meanwhile, the use of an inexhaustible solar and geothermal energy potential is insufficient.

The scientific problem is the evaluation of the social utility of RES that can demonstrate the advantages which are underestimated in investment decisions (Strantzali and Aravossis 2015). The most important benefits are the inexhaustibility of RES and the possibility of ensuring sufficient energy resources for future generations. The utilisation of certain RES technologies, such as solar energy, helps to solve environmental issues as well. Therefore, RES may be additionally financed from other sources. The main issue is the diversity of RES utilisation opportunities and incentives. Moreover, it is a transfer of certain economic interpretations on uniform rules and economic laws into a specified dimension, in this case trying to reduce different opinions as much as possible.

Arcos, Gomez and Garcia (2019) proposed a methodology that, using only publicly available information, assesses the capacity of urban agglomerations to be self-sufficient and energy sustainable. The methodology evaluates the potential of the urban surface to accommodate thermal and PV solar facilities, as well as the energy storage requirements on a year-round basis.

> When applied to the city of Seville, considering not only the current electricity demand but also the one arising from the electrification of both urban transport and the entire thermal energy currently supplied by gas, the conclusion is that it is possible to have a self-supplied energy system based almost exclusively on PV and thermal panels. Given the high cost of seasonal storage, the resulting system is economically unviable, so it makes sense to keep the transmission grid as a back-up system to feed power into the city at certain times of the year (up to 8% of annual consumption). In the

case study, the renewable energy comes mainly from PV facilities roof-mounted (72%), or ground-mounted in the surrounding urban lots (25%), plus a modest contribution from biogas (wastewater) (Arcos, Gomez and Garcia 2019).

The inexhaustibility of RES could change the use of fossil fuels, such as oil and natural gas, and replace them with different types of energy. This could be solar, wind, and geothermal energy. On the other hand, the social utility of RES differs from oil and natural gas, because RES guarantees the supply of energy resources for future generations, although this benefit does not have a methodological evaluation. This is one of the keys to the concept of sustainable energy development.

If direct support is applied for RES or environmental technologies, the impact would depend on the volume of support and the source of funding. For example, if direct assistance is financed from the state budget, the promotion measures would increase the budget deficit in addition to the abovementioned positive aspects. It is, therefore, essential that the promotion is cost-effective: the benefits should exceed the negative effects. Inexhaustible types of RES (wind, solar, and geothermal energy) enable greater benefit than potential subsidies required while penetration into the market is growing.

Balancing RES support forms as the substance for the spatial planning method

Different types of RES have a very broad and distinctive scale of use; therefore, each renewable requires its own specific support. This topic has focused on the potential analysis of wind, solar, and geothermal energy for small-scale applications.

Support measures for the use of RES often contradict market patterns due to short-term period goals, which are one of the main disadvantages in nearly all countries. These measures do not shape uniform technological programmes for long-term periods. The EU document (European Commission, 2013) on establishing support schemes for RES technologies defines the necessity of revising current RES support measures which cause market failures, e.g. the feed-in tariff increases the supply, however, it also increases electricity and heat tariffs for all consumers. Therefore, this initiates constant changes in the support measures, which, as a result, causes instability and, thus, distortion of the investment environment.

Every renewable has a wide and developing scale of technologies which are becoming cheaper due to the growth of supply. Also, each renewable has a different significance in terms of external benefit, thus, support schemes can differ significantly. This depends on the environmental situation in various areas. External conditions and current infrastructure, where RES technologies could be applied, differ as well; therefore, spatial planning is the most appropriate tool for assessment via urban energy development plans.

Most countries mainly support RES technologies on the supply side, while opportunities to use solar energy are significant on the consumers' side, e.g. as small systems of solar collectors in multi-apartment buildings. Support for consumers is the most appropriate via support programmes, and not by supporting scattered consumers, as programmes enable the actual effect to be achieved. Renovation of buildings by districts enables planned actions, which could solve technical and financial problems for DH companies due to reduced consumption. The law on RES of the Republic of Lithuania includes several statements dedicated to the individual consumption of RES using energy generators. However, such schemes as feed-in tariffs, green certificates, auctions, etc., which are applied in Lithuania, are adopted for companies implementing small-scale projects with respective competencies. Applying the above schemes for small producers increases administration costs and is often not acceptable due to the high level of complexity. Therefore, territorial administration is needed.

The periodisation of the economic age and the assessment of various different RES support forms, with regard to the specifics, has different goals and tasks from a macroeconomic point of view. Short-term, medium-term, and long-term goals and respective motivation systems for various RES technologies are presented in this section. Domination of the few RES in power and heat generation is an evident shortcoming related to the short-term perspective (which reflects the new EU support period). Large imported wind plants dominate in terms of power generation, though small PV, wind, and various hybrid plants would have a wider application in the medium and long-term perspective.

The main problem is that programmes for the implementation of legally delegated functions have no consolidating unity. This causes serious problems, e.g. renovation of multi-apartment residential houses would reduce the heat consumption significantly, and, therefore, would cause the growth of DH tariffs due to the growing fixed heat generation and supply costs. A stable and balanced programme with carefully selected subsidising, enabling interaction between the consumers and heat suppliers, is necessary to solve these problems.

Certain types of RES differ in various aspects, thus, classification based on renewability is important for the assessment of possibilities and for the justification of respective economic measures in terms of future implementation. The important disadvantage is that RES assessment and implementation takes place in the short-term period, relating to the EU support period up to 2020. This is the reason why only biomass and wind plants are dominating in heat and power generation sectors in Lithuania. Therefore, short-term (until 2020) and medium-term (until 2030) periods are important. The Danish example shows that prospective vision (until 2050) is also possible. A well-developed infrastructure of DH systems and spatial planning systems is very important for the assessment of complex effects and practical implementation. Solar energy can be used for both power and heat generation. The scale of technologies is wide, and the dynamics of competitiveness is different bearing in mind the reduction of technological costs during the time. The use of solar collectors for the production of hot tap water in multi-apartment buildings is already competitive. In the long run, all RES technologies should be evaluated not only as competing with each other but also as being able to gradually replace fossil fuel. The rapid replacement of a certain technology is impossible: solar energy can be used during the limited summer period, and the volumes of heat generation are not large, while the use of wind energy depends on climate conditions. Scattered generation characteristics, and the fact that most of the installations of such type can be implemented on the demand side, are left to private initiatives. With regard to involving hardly competitive energy sources, an investment management institution is required. Municipalities could act as institutions seeking the development of wide-scale RES technologies. Actual legislation in Lithuania shows that municipal powers and responsibilities regarding RES are regulated in detail. There are no barriers, except for financing issues relating to municipalities' actions. Some of them have signed the Covenant of Mayors; some have adopted RES development action plans, however, only a few of them are really taking action.

Each RES has a different value in terms of external benefit, thus, respective promotion schemes can and must differ significantly. This depends on the environmental situation in a certain area. External conditions and current infrastructure for RES technologies differ, thus, spatial planning is the most appropriate tool for assessment of the benefit, e.g. urban energy development plans. All countries pay little attention to the support of RES technologies on the demand side. Support for consumers is the most effective via programmes, rather than at the individual consumer level, as it provides the potential to achieve the actual effect. Evaluation is performed based on the methodology presented above.

However, the balancing of various RES implementation aspects is still important. Development stages are maximised based on the technological indicators (share of RES in power and heat sectors), economic indicators (change of created added value and investment volumes) and social indicators (employment or new jobs) and minimised, based on environmental indicators (the least impact assessed using the index of sustainable progress). The target function was formed with regard to the integrated sustainable development assessment methodology used by Čiegis (2010). Optimisation of the existing energy infrastructure forms the short-term stage for energy sector development. Introduction of new energy technologies and smart grid control systems into the programme forms the long-term stage. The formation of stages can be performed via investment limitations. The case of modelling can be used for planning investments, using Lithuanian and EU funding for RES development. In the case of unlimited investment in the energy sector, the focus on the promotion of technological innovations in energy generation, using new sources in energy production and regarding ecological, social and energy efficiency criteria is required.

Growing fossil fuel prices due to the introduction of hidden costs and social taxes would stimulate social-economic development, thus leading to faster development of RES actions, infrastructure and energy generation technologies (Duer and Christensen 2010).

Proper assessment of taxes and costs helps RES to compete with fossil fuel, however, market stakeholders are not interested in the price, but rather in the stability and ability to forecast, which would provide a background to invest into energy-saving measures, thus reducing total energy expenses. If the saving of one kilowatt-hour costs less than generating it, investment should be directed not towards the installation of new capacities, but to the saving of the secondary energy, thus providing energy services at the lowest costs. Investment should be directed where it provides the highest effect, and investment into energy-saving measures is often more beneficial from an economic as well as an environmental point of view (Klevas 2010) and (Klevas 2012).

CHAPTER THREE

THE FRAMEWORK FOR SUSTAINABLE SPATIAL ENERGY PROGRAMMES

The ongoing energy transition processes need a rapprochement between the places of energy production and consumption to create innovative and integrated territorial models. Consequently, models and strategies for increasing the use of local and RES play a key role in enhancing energy independence and the sustainability of the considered areas. A very good example is presented by Santolini, Mancini and Garcia (2019).

> The main objective of this study is to analyse the energy system of the Lazio Region in Italy, comparing electricity consumptions and production from renewable sources at the municipality scale. In order to estimate the electricity consumptions and the local production by RES, the main sectors of electricity consumption together with the potential of the available RES for electricity production have been analysed. The obtained results pinpointed the main critical aspects of the Lazio region, that are mainly focalized in the city of Rome and in the most densely inhabited municipalities. Furthermore, research outputs provide an overall framework on the regional RES potential and allowed the formulation of proposals aimed at overcoming the identified criticalities and increasing the share of electricity production from renewables. Finally, the research approach could be replicated in other areas, providing a useful process for decision-makers and stakeholders (Santolini, Mancini and Garcia 2019).

Analysis of the energy sector and the stages of its development in Lithuania are investigated using the process network synthesis (PNS) method, with an overview of the best examples in EU member states.

Formation of energy sector development stages is based on the following statements:

1. Gradual reduction of the use of fossil fuel and respective increase of the use of RES with regard to RES action plans in cities or regions.
2. Formation of energy sector development plans, seeking to achieve the major share of RES in total energy production by 2020.

3. Formation of long-term energy sector development via the use of RES for energy generation, and residual energy transfer to power grids; development of DH networks using smart grid technologies.

The following stages of energy sector development are investigated:

1) **The short-term** development stage includes the period until the year 2020. This is a RES programme, aiming to implement planned RES indicators for the energy sector with rather moderate financing and technical tools. This is the stage of optimisation of the energy sector structure, including reforming the DH sector, promoting small-scale modernisation in the heat sector, and replacing the use of fossil fuel technologies with RES technologies. In fact, this is the optimisation of the currently existing energy system in terms of gradual modernisation and wider use of feasible RES technologies.

2) **The long-term** energy sector development stage is after the year 2020. This is the stage of optimal use of RES and smart grids, when the existing energy system is reorganised via the implementation of smart energy technologies, enabling wider use of RES: solar, wind, and geothermal, aiming to maximise the RES energy supply.

Short-term period (until 2020). This stage of energy sector development is already being implemented according to the national RES measures in the action plan, using national and EU financial support. This period envisages a wider use of biomass for energy generation. This means the development of biomass in the DH sector by replacing existing natural gas boilers with biomass installations. Decentralised heat generation envisages the modernisation of thermal installations. Heat installations using low-quality forest wood and wood waste are to be replaced by a more efficient system using wood pellets or briquettes. The use of natural gas is unrestricted, however, the change in prices of natural gas and biomass enables the use of PNS, which provides the feasibility estimate.

Analysing the short-term period until the year 2020 using PNS optimises the use of decentralised heating in the energy sectors, taking into account the changes in natural gas, biofuels and biomass prices, the growth of the biomass supply, biogas production technologies with regard to used resources and price, and the price of biogas. Bearing this in mind, three development scenarios can be formed for the second short-term stage of energy sector development:

1. The first option investigates the changes in biomass resource volumes on the supply and demand side, compared to the basic resources of the status quo stage.
2. The second option investigates possibilities of using other RES, with an optimal ratio of biomass on the supply and demand side.

3. The third option investigates changes in the energy sector due to the change in natural gas prices.

This stage requires modelling based on smart grid development, providing the possibility to design electricity and heat transmission and distribution networks, systems and technologies, which will enable producers and consumers to exchange energy (Yadav et al. 2019). In such a system, energy consumers and energy producers can transfer energy and sell to other consumers, depending on energy demand. User-installed upstream energy generation, storage and balancing technologies guarantee the security of energy supply, while the use of energy with automatic distribution technologies controls the energy exchange process.

> The long-term development stage envisages the implementation of excess energy storage, transmission, balancing and reservation, via the use of RES technologies. Farming and forest-based solid biomass fuel resources can be stored during the entire year, while solar and wind energy is best to use on an instant basis, which may increase the energy shortages. The future is for energy generation on both sides—supply and demand—as well as trade between both sides using smart grids (Colak et al. 2015).

The main idea of such a system is the energy exchange process directly between producer and consumer using smart grid technologies. The development of smart grids enables efficient energy distribution provided by producers and suppliers, thus improving energy efficiency and reducing energy losses in networks. Besides, smart grids reduce CO_2 emissions and establish conditions for the development of modern grid energy systems, enabling the operation of decentralised energy distribution.

This process increases the variety of energy generation technologies and energy resources. Smart grids optimally distribute energy resources, as this depends on technologies and consumers' demands. Appropriate solutions in grid energy systems should be found by the application of stage-based programmes, thus avoiding mistakes and moving the energy sector in the appropriate direction.

Lithuanian legislation regarding self-government provides a fairly broad scale of opportunities for this kind of prospective planning to improve energy efficiency and the use of RES. The law on Local Self-Government distinguishes autonomous municipal functions, e.g., elaborating the municipal strategic plans and secondary documents, as well as implementing these plans. The law on Renewable Energy defines the measures to elaborate plans for the development of RES. Municipalities also administer the implementation of the Rural Development Programme. The Self-Government Act stipulates that municipalities organise the supply of heat in their area, while the Heat Sector Law regulates special heat planning as a mechanism for the implementation of this obligation. Besides, the role of municipalities in apartment building renovation has noticeably increased in the past few years.

Therefore, a particularly important recommendation is the arrangement of large-scale training for municipal energy planners. It would be appropriate to develop a model methodology for a municipal energy development plan (short-term and long-term), linking to the consolidation of financial resources for its implementation. It is necessary to form not only short-term but also long-term municipal and district heat supply development scenarios using renewable technologies. Otherwise, only one-sided scenarios are possible with the domination of the cheapest fuels. After several years of price changes, plans and scenarios for adjustments are required.

CHAPTER FOUR

RES TECHNOLOGY IMPLEMENTATION IN ECO-VILLAGES AND GREEN SETTLEMENTS

The promotion of RES on a wider scale was implemented in the EU by creating green settlements or so-called eco-villages (Bayulken and Huisingh 2014). The state-funded project "Climate Menu" in the Netherlands enabled towns to select sectors which need exceptional attention in order to meet national obligations. Environmental policy is implemented by towns, as the best possibilities are concentrated there and the issues are most visible in these areas. The share of the subsidy assigned to a certain municipality depends on its area and population, thus smaller municipalities co-operate and implement joint projects, enabling them to save money. There are approximately 500 municipalities in the Netherlands—300 of them have already had support. Each town, depending on scale, organisational skills and specifics, could promote its areas of activity. State subsidies can cover 50% of the total project implementation costs, and the rest is covered by the municipality itself. Each municipality selects the financing sector. There are three levels of goals which show the level at which the municipality intends to develop the funded area. State-funded projects should be implemented over four years. The use of RES is similarly promoted in Austria. Every municipality selects individual support measures and financial tools aimed at promoting the development of RES technologies. Mainly, these are solar technologies and the modernisation of DH systems using biomass.

The idea of eco-villages and research on the concept, as well as creating strategies and finding specific solutions for problem-solving, has been analysed over the last decades of the twentieth century all over the world. For further information, see Takeuchi, Namiki and Tanaka (1998) and Marckmann, Gram-Hanssen and Christensen (2012); for planning, see Cheng and Hu (2010) and Zheng and Gao (2013); for design and construction, see Hu and Wang (1998); and for assessing sustainability, see Barton (2000). Modelling methods were used for resources management and sustainability assessment (Harmaajärvi 2000). The most recent research concentrates on eco-innovations, eco-efficiency and eco-effectiveness

(Carrillo-Hermosilla 2012), and cultivation of eco-sustainability on various social-economic-environmental levels (Wang et al. 2011). The investigations also involve the role of eco-cultural diversity (Hong 2011), renewable energy in eco-communities (Rae and Bradley), and understanding the eco-complexity and ecosystem approach (Wang et al. 2010).

The global movement of green settlements appears to be very important. It was initiated at the UN-Habitat declaration in 1976. This idea has become rational and effective in various aspects and energy use was one of the most significant ones. Following the principles of Agenda 21 accepted at the Rio Summit in 1992, the baseline of sustainable development for settlements was adopted and, finally, the essential principles were adopted at the Un-Habitat II conference in Istanbul in 1996.

Declarations on the sustainable development of settlements state that cities and settlements were and are the incubators of our civilisation and generators of growth, which have accelerated the evolution of knowledge, culture and traditions, as well as industry and trade. Properly planned and controlled urban settlements create favourable perspectives for human development and the protection of global natural resources.

Eco-villages or green settlements are driven by local initiatives, local communities and group leaders in pursuit of the following main objectives: to create a better, healthier, eco-friendlier lifestyle, to foster a social and community lifestyle, and to encourage the development of an ecological permaculture and a natural economy.

According to the data of the international organisation, "Global Eco-Village Network", there are more than 40,000 ecological villages around the world. A movement of ecological villages is usually driven by local community initiatives, however, more often it is supported by governmental subsidies. For example, the British Government has accepted and supported the construction and development programme of four new eco-villages (Lithuanian Republic Ministry of Agriculture 2008). The main problem is the supply of energy resources which still exists in rural areas. The main question, emphasising the actuality of this scientific work, is to connect various research results into a united and practically applied model of green settlements, covering the criteria of sustainable development.

The use of green energy is one of the top priorities in the projects of green settlements developed by local communities. A separate group, considering thermal and electrical energy production and consumption, has been formed. The optimal use of RES and effective energy consumption are the main aspects of the formation of a model of green settlements. There are no directives and legal norms which regulate the development of green settlements, therefore, the development of such settlements is considered a local initiative, driven mostly by local leaders and using the bottom-up approach.

The energy model of green settlements includes the formation of electricity, heat production and consumption scenarios, where the use of local and renewable sources is considered. The formation of an energy model for green settlements assumes that the share of RES should be not less than that mentioned in the Directive on the promotion of the use of RES. The prospective development of green settlements cannot be suspended by the year 2020. Preferably, an assumption is accepted that the model of green settlements must be based on using 100% of RES in the future in the optimal case. This technical target is just a guideline, as other factors, e.g. economic, social and environmental, also need to be included. Therefore, the development of green settlements is a never-ending, continuous process, similar to the cycles of nature, where forms of energy change one another. It is important to scientifically justify the systematic use of renewable sources, perform the flow analysis for the reserves and waste management, using resources. It is necessary to develop a secondary use of resources, where the toxic waste is involved in the technical (anthropogenic) and biological (ecosphere) cycle. The green settlement is primarily related to the understanding of the ecosystem and the holistic approach to the formation of an ecological lifestyle. Living organisms and their environmental interactions in nature are interdependent processes that work together ensuring the life and convenience of the system (Palojarvi 2013). Therefore, the development of the green settlement model is intended to preserve the entity of nature and to emphasise the dependent position for each of its parts and humanity as well.

The principle of the ecological movement can be expressed by the quote "think globally, act locally". Progress in solving environmental problems can be achieved more quickly if the principles of our activities and the functions of natural law systems are harmonised (Kalenda 2007). This was the main principle of the development of green settlements. The energy sector of green settlements duplicates the processes in nature which is a perfect example of waste-free technology. The volume of waste generated in the energy sector can be reduced by increasing the efficiency of the use of primary energy sources, promoting the use of RES, and choosing eco-friendly products and materials with components less harmful to the environment. The negative impact on the environment can be mitigated through more efficient use of RES in the energy sector developed under the circular economy model and bioregional development principles. The use of RES in the regions can create a unique environment for resource utilisation (Birekland 2008). The exploitation of energy resources must not exceed the resilience limits of nature, otherwise, RES can be treated as non-renewable resources. The development of the regional energy sector according to the principles of the circular economy is encouraging the use of a wide range of local and renewable resources. The concept of the circular economy has been investigated by Andersen (2006), Bartl (2015), Guohui and Yunfeng (2012), Geng et al. (2011), Wu et al. (2013) and the cradle-to-cradle development approach by Braungart, McDonough and Bollinger (2007), McDonough et al. (2003), and van Dijk, Tenpierik and van den Dobbelsteen (2013). The approach regarding implementing green settlements has been analysed in Lithuania as well (Klevas, Biekša and Murauskaitė 2014).

A green settlement is like a living laboratory where ecological innovations are created and solutions are accepted ensuring sustainable development in the sector of civil engineering, energy use, waste and wastewater management, transport, agriculture and food production, and the culture of consumption. The PNS method is applied for research in this "laboratory". The PNS method is associated with the creation of the algorithm which helps to conceptualise the present situation and to forecast options of feasible decisions, as well as helping to identify what kind of information is necessary in order to evaluate the consequences of the decision-making.

PART V

PROSPECTS FOR THE HARMONIOUS DEVELOPMENT OF ENERGY

CHAPTER ONE

ADDRESSING THE CHALLENGE OF ENERGY SECURITY FOR FUTURE GENERATIONS IN THE CONTEXT OF THE KNOWLEDGE ECONOMY CONCEPT

Assumptions regarding economic policy

The aspiration of humanity to "conquer Nature" and subordinate it for its economic goals has obviously failed. Natural disasters are a continuous reminder of this, and the sceptics' voices regarding allegedly unrelated natural phenomena are being suppressed in the face of obvious facts.

In any case, the new paradigm for harmonious progress must be realised in one form or another in economic policy. These policies must emerge from previous theories, which we will briefly discuss in this section.

Returning to the development of RES technologies and their wider use, business support policies and measures need to be linked to improving the competitiveness of domestic companies, stimulating innovation, and analysing each individual case. The modern state must also regulate the business in terms of external factors that will affect future generations. In all cases, all circumstances must be assessed. However, addressing negative externalities requires restraint rather than encouragement, while positive externalities cannot be effectively addressed by the market alone. Competitiveness is most effectively enhanced by promoting basic research and knowledge dissemination, which is already a form of indirect business support, as these functions are usually performed by research institutes.

When assessing the preconditions for the support of RES for business and consumers, the most commonly mentioned ones are pollution taxes. However, in the current economic climate, the issue of taxes and other economic and fiscal instruments is becoming much more complex due to the need to harmonise international aspects in a globally competitive environment. The negative effects of taxation include relocating polluting industries to countries with less stringent environmental requirements, rather than introducing innovations that reduce pollution. In the meantime, a country with high taxes and "green tax reform" may not reduce its pollution if the pollution company moves to a neighbouring country, and at the same time does not collect the necessary taxes. For these reasons, and for the sake of competitiveness in general, countries are reluctant to apply the penalty principle to polluters and to provide support for better, environmentally friendly operators to increase their competitiveness, otherwise, the scales would shift to using RES, such as wind energy.

In conclusion, taxes and support are not entirely adequate instruments to address the challenges of sustainable development. In my opinion, measures to stimulate the demand for RES are of particular importance. At the very least, there must be a balance between supply and demand. This is where the principles of knowledge structure formation should come into play, but it is necessary to form them in a unified methodological way.

Lack of sufficient capital on the domestic front necessitates the attraction of foreign investment—the incoming investment is in the interest of more productive work for the employees, which also results in the introduction of new technologies. Protectionism does not attract more citizens or foreign capital through production subsidies; these measures can only channel capital from one branch to another. Thus, it is not the protectionist policies of local producers but the capital raising policies that can enhance the well-being of a country. In the study by Klevas (2015), it was proven that certain elements of economic support for the use of RES technologies must be based on the usefulness of RES as regards environmental protection, as well as economic and social aspects.

Renewable energy policies are being implemented to promote the diffusion of RES within the market. However, their effectiveness as regards their renewable electricity capacity remains uncertain. The study of Nurcan Kilinc-Ata addresses the most effective renewable policy instruments to increase the capacity of RES. This study employs a 1990-2008 panel dataset to conduct an econometric analysis of policy instruments, namely, feed-in tariffs, quotas, tenders and tax incentives, in promoting renewable energy deployment in 27 EU countries and 50 US states.

> The results suggest that renewable energy policy instruments play a significant role in encouraging RES, but their effectiveness differs by type of renewable energy policy instruments. Findings reveal that feed-in tariffs, tenders and tax incentives are effective mechanisms for stimulating deployment capacity of RES for electricity, while the other commonly used policy instrument—quota—is not (Kilinc-Ata 2019).

However, the method in this study does not allow the author to state which economic policy is the most effective. A more precise and rational evaluation method would be the analysis of the influence of aggregated political instruments.

The investigation provided by Liu, Zhang and Feng develops a fixed-effect model to evaluate the effect of renewable energy policy using a panel dataset covering 29 countries between 2000 and 2015. The renewable energy policy system in this investigation includes seven aggregate policies and 12 specific ones.

> The empirical results indicate that four of seven aggregate policies, including fiscal and financial incentives, market-based instruments, policy support, and research, development and deployment, are demonstrated to be significant to the improvement of renewable energy capacity. Meanwhile, three of 12 specific policies, including price policy, grants and subsidies, and strategic planning, have positive effects on renewable energy development. The investigation assesses the aggregate and specific policies in the same analysis framework, and the empirical results determined that synergy effects existed among specific policies. The empirical results also indicate that the implementation of the Kyoto Protocol in 2005 has had positive impacts on renewable energy development in typical countries (Liu, Zhang and Feng 2019).

But it is one thing to state the facts and another to justify their economic substance. Standard market economists (I call them market fundamentalists) protest against any support they believe is exceptional and complain about unequal market conditions. However, the essence of what we have already discussed in the previous section is the external efficiency of RES technologies.

What is known as prosperity economics was initiated by A. Marshall (1961), who was the first to use the terms "external economy" and "external diseconomy" and noted the limitations of the market mechanism. In economic theory, the term "external effect" has become established. External effects are the added benefits to the production or consumption of a good or the harm caused to businesses or individuals who are neither producers nor consumers of that good; Mansfield (1979), Nureev (2000) and Friedman (1998) describe it as a "neighbourhood problem". Thus, externalities show the difference between social and private costs or benefits. And this, according to Pigou (1932), requires the intervention of the state: the state must regulate the market for goods through taxes and subsidies.

In the neoclassical economy, there is a strong emphasis on welfare, which makes the theory of welfare economics distinct. The concept of public welfare has already been formulated by J. Bentham, stating that the aim of politics must be "the greatest happiness for the greatest number".

Thus, the welfare economy seeks a way of distributing resources within society that maximises overall prosperity and produces the greatest societal benefits. However, the optimum achieved in the market does not necessarily coincide with the "social" optimality (Degutis 1998). Thus, according to this theory, the well-being of a community, rather than of its separate individuals, plays a key role. It is assumed that the more evenly distributed wealth is in society, the greater the overall well-being. Prosperity economics justifies market intervention, providing social support to the most deprived, including support for small and medium-sized businesses and justifying support for farmers as rural populations tend to be poorer than those in urban areas.

The mathematical school (except for Pareto) positively evaluated state interventionism—not due to the greater support for entrepreneurs, but, on the contrary, entrepreneurs would share more of their welfare with their employees. Such a redistributive objective is related to the welfare economy.

Pigou (1932), argued that conflicts can arise between private and public interests. More importantly, conflicts can arise between the benefits of the present moment and the interests of future generations. These conflicts are related to public goods and externalities, e.g. pollution caused by the burning of fuels to produce energy, the consequences of which will be felt not only now but also in the future.

Inefficiencies in the allocation of productive resources result from the production (or consumption) in society of too many goods with negative externalities and too few goods with positive externalities (Nureev 2000). An example of a positive external effect is when a landfill is cleaned up and the gas that accumulates is not only released into the environment but also used to produce energy—heat. External effects, both negative and positive, are excluded from market relationships. Those who receive additional benefits do not contribute to the cost of creating those benefits, and those who suffer from negative externalities are not compensated. Market foreclosure results from the poor ability and motivation of the decision-maker to bear the costs or benefits of externalities. For example, polluting companies have no incentive to reduce emissions unless they know they can participate in emissions trading. But this system does not solve the global problem of pollution, so it merely redistributes the pollution between states, which is a flawed solution in the context of the Paris Agreement.

Many scholars, for example, Samuelson (1983) and Nureev (2000), distinguish two main policies: the commercialisation of the public goods market and state intervention. They prefer the latter route.

Both measures—public intervention and commercialisation—aim to internalise externalities into the cost and thus manage supply and demand. Internalisation is "the process of using many mechanisms that encourage decision-makers to weigh external costs and benefits before making decisions" (Coase 1992; 1995).

Formation of the educational programme

By analysing the growth of the importance of knowledge in the development processes, A. Burton-Jones (1999) highlights the concept of knowledge capitalism. The concept of knowledge capitalism expresses the idea that the key to the accumulation of capital for man, and thus, for society, is not the available wealth, but the available knowledge capital. For these reasons, social welfare is not increased by redistributing money, taxes and business support. A person or an entrepreneur would earn much more if he had better knowledge and qualifications and used them properly (as having knowledge does not guarantee better application). The only question to be debated is whether the state should care about people's knowledge or leave it to self-education.

V. Snitka (2002) notes that the main emphasis should be placed not on what products Lithuania uses to compete, but how Lithuania competes. Only new, intelligent and high-quality products or services are expensive. Exporting high-productivity, competitive firms raises labour costs in the state, increases economic efficiency and capital, and reduces the competitiveness of other industries.

The country's competitiveness in a post-capitalist society can be defined as having high productivity, which generates high income for the people and the state budget, and at the same time ensures better social guarantees in the country. In this case, using the concept of the knowledge economy, it can be argued that in order to cope with international competition, capital and labour need to be redirected towards high value-added industries. Such a position is similar to the "educative protectionism" proposed by the German Historical School—supporting a young national industry until it reaches maturity.

Another scholar, Krugman (1996), has criticised "educative protectionism", arguing that markets themselves are best placed to decide which innovation is commercially viable. However, it should be noted that the dissemination of knowledge is linked to the latest scientific research. Government research support is not a direct form of support for business or industry. Although research funding is usually classified as a separate branch of support (R. Vilpišauskas 2004), this is not correct. It is incorrect to relate it solely to sectorial support. Although the diffusion of innovations rarely occurred in the industrial society, the situation has changed in the post-industrial society. Drucker researched innovation and the question of the diffusion of technological progress (Drucker 2004) and noted that if innovative products, e.g. transistors, were being developed for one industry (the phone industry), they were thought to be limited and applicable only to this industry. However, the opposite has happened—this particular innovation has received a more competitive application in a completely different industry—the computer industry. Thus, public support for innovative research and knowledge dissemination do not need to be confined to one distinct sector, but rather to a number of industries (which might be unpredictable). The support for the dissemination of knowledge can also be combined with horizontal support (without distinguishing between individual branches of the economy supported).

However, not all government support for research into innovation and knowledge dissemination is to be classified as horizontal support. Support is horizontal if there are equal possibilities for the diffusion of innovation between different branches of the economy. V. Snitka (2002) emphasised that research into innovation can be divided into three types, according to the potential to create economic value through knowledge dissemination, which is related to the possibility of the diffusion of innovation. Basic research is usually carried out in universities or other research institutions where research is not commercially oriented. Applied research is a continuation of basic research, but it already has a commercial purpose in mind. Product development involves a field of research that is directly related to the development of a real commercial product.

Since basic research generates the knowledge upon which all commercial applications are based, the results belonging to the general public, the dissemination of basic research cannot be restricted. Results are widely publicised and must be publicly funded. State support for product development research is thus the least justified. Most of the public interest can be attributed to the promotion of basic research (since the knowledge created here is non-patentable and accessible to all). Knowledge, gained from basic research, can be equated to a public good, and, therefore, support for the production and dissemination of this type of knowledge can have a positive effect on a country's competitiveness.

F. A. von Hayek defined the subject, goals and objectives of economic science according to the principle of limited knowledge. For example, he explored the problem of making the best use of resources (not of the distribution), the relative value of which is known only to individuals themselves, or, in short, the "use of knowledge not provided to any separate individual".

One of the major tasks of economics, for this economist, was to find out how different human behaviour results in a sufficiently rigid social order. According to F. A. von Hayek, the order can be created deliberately or in a spontaneous way. The specificity of spontaneous order is that it is not the realisation of ideas, but rather the evolutionary path of the natural process of social development, as a natural result of the conscious action of many people. Spontaneous order is the result of human actions, not the product of the human mind. According to F. A. von Hayek:

> The present order of society did not result from purposeful efforts, but rather from the progressive establishment of more efficient institutions through competition. Rather, the structures formed by traditions were due to the "sifting" process, propelled by the benefits that groups gain by adopting—for unknown or perhaps purely accidental reasons—a particular way of behaving (Hayek 1967).

F. A. von Hayek demonstrated that knowledge, accumulated in society as habits, traditions and norms, is transmitted through upbringing and usually adopted without a real understanding of the meaning of certain norms, but this does not diminish their relevance to society.

It is clear that the use of RES is the flagship of all sustainable development. However, mass utilisation is only possible by radically reforming the educational system, even human mentality, and eventually revising the basic postulates of economic theory. As stated by the famous philosopher and psychologist, E. Fromm (2008):

> Psychological reasoning is an important stimulus leading to certain conclusions. We can go even further and assert that ideas, that are not rooted in the immediate needs of the personality, will have very little effect on human behaviour and his life.

To supplement this statement about the paradigm of harmonious progress of energetics, the following author can be quoted again:

> The influence of any doctrine or idea depends on the degree to which it corresponds to the psychology of the people for whom the idea is intended. An idea can become an active force in history only if it meets the immediate psychological needs of certain social groups (Fromm 2008).

Supporting the demand for renewable energy is not—and cannot be—an isolated task in the context of a unified energy policy. However, only the motivation for economic support is of real use and not the pursuit of set targets at all costs. Unmotivated social utility promotion can steer the market mechanism in the wrong direction and disorganise market participants. In the context of energy economics, it is clear that support for RES is needed, as the market mechanism cannot provide sufficient impetus for their penetration into the market (Sonenblum 1978). This is due to the enormous environmental damage, generally referred to as external costs, caused by the burning of conventional fuels—coal, petroleum products and natural gas—that are not reflected in the price. As a result, support measures are required. More importantly, the market does not capture the positive effects on the environment and the social welfare that can be gained from the widespread use of RES.

The paradigm of harmonious progress significantly extends the general notion of economic development and accordingly sets new goals and assumptions which are described in Fig. 5-1.

Fig. 5-1 illustrates the essence and principles of economic support for knowledge generation based on the evaluation of the social utility of RES.

The education system is only one part of a complex and long-term process (Hargreaves and Goodson 2006). In the short, medium and long term, the emphasis should be placed on teaching, continuously improving the education system and conducting research.

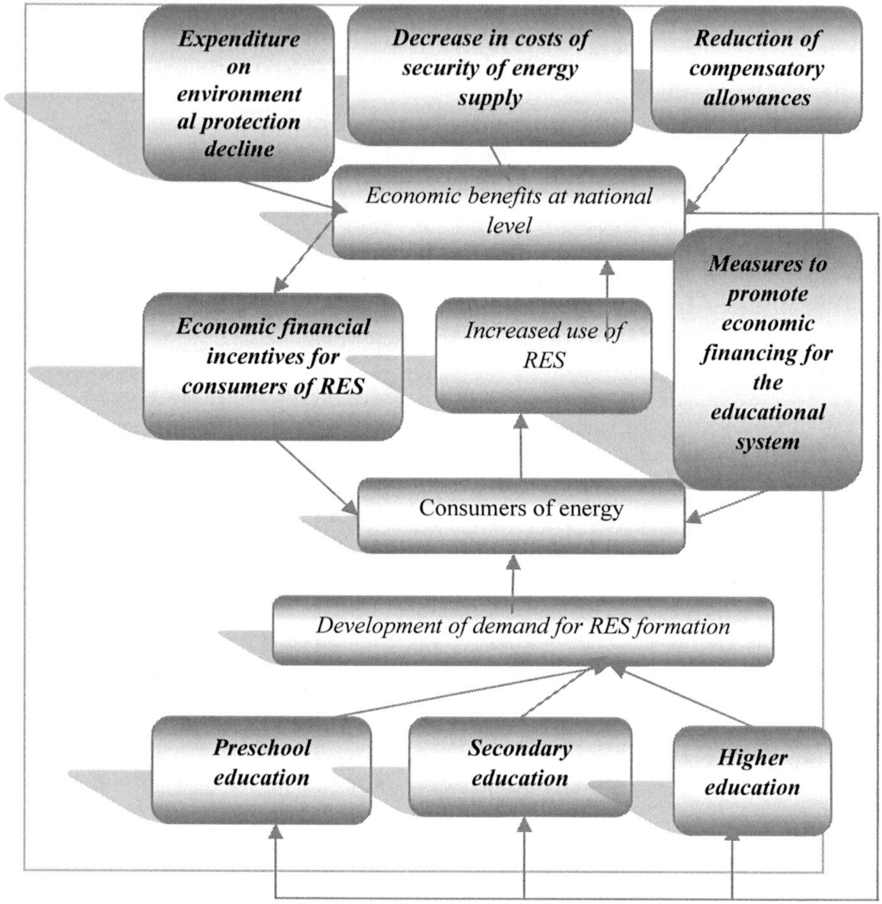

Fig. 5-1. Motives for the development of the demand for sustainable energy innovations using the example of RES

The concept and characterisation of municipal knowledge as a non-competitive organisation in the use of renewable energy technologies

From the point of view of the subject matter, it is particularly important to study how individual knowledge can and must be transformed into organisational knowledge, and how this knowledge can be managed. The answers to these questions are sought by both management researchers and business organisations. The thoughts and generalisations of Chen and Dahlman (2004) are particularly informative, generalising, and capable of becoming a solid base for our statements. The authors have analysed the positions in the scientific literature that are not general in terms of knowledge management. This and other articles explain how to create, share, and use knowledge in order to transform individual knowledge into organisational knowledge. The subject of the research is the management of individual and organisational knowledge. The paper reviews knowledge management models that could be applied in Lithuanian companies and would guarantee effective knowledge creation, dissemination and use. The authors follow the approach of Despres and Chauvel (2004), which suggests distinguishing between two types of knowledge—individual and organisational. One of the main goals of the organisation should be the transformation of individual and non-formal knowledge into defined organisational knowledge. The main reason for this transformation is that the knowledge defined by the organisation can be replicated and used many times. However, this and other studies of this type emphasise the competitiveness of an organisation seeking profit as a key driver and motive for turning individual knowledge into organisational knowledge.

However, there are organisations which, by their nature and constitutional responsibility, do not consider profits derived from statistical methods but the well-being and ecological status of the people living in the area, including socially responsible entrepreneurs, in supporting progress in the welfare of the state. Transforming the concept of knowledge economics for this type of organisation is yet another challenge.

The best example of this trend in the development of the knowledge economy is the increase in RES utilisation. Local authorities clearly have a significant role to play in the implementation process. The results of our previous multidisciplinary analysis (Klevas 2015) reveal that it is only territorially possible to demonstrate what is underestimated in business terms—namely, public benefits in various aspects that are impossible or very difficult to evaluate from an individual business point of view. For example, the use of RES, wind and geothermal technologies is not being exploited to the appropriate extent, because there is no other way of demonstrating their social usefulness, other than the social-environmental aspirations of a given area, which should be pursued by the municipal administration. Therefore, a new scientific problem arises, in essence, defining a different type of knowledge of organisations, which is not aimed at increasing the competitiveness of an organisation compared to others, but its efficiency and ability to organise and apply knowledge for the welfare of the state and society. As the description of all municipal functions would be extremely broad and overly complex, we use the example of how individual knowledge within a municipality can be organised to increase the competitiveness of the energy system—RES—compared to conventional energy sources, combustion of which is generally recognised as a "producer" of climate change initiating gas. The breakthrough of RES technologies in the market is too narrowly perceived as the mass use of biofuels in the municipally controlled area. The article (Klevienė 2011) noted the special feature of RES technologies that allegedly contradict economic regularities, namely, that the increase in their demand lowers the price of these technologies (as opposed to the case of limited resources). This knowledge does not create competitive advantages. Its widespread diffusion increases the demand for RES technologies and is a major driver of production.

The key issue is to achieve, through long-term policy, a situation where various types of RES find a niche for their long-term application, which, in essence, implies the stability of energy prices and the guarantee of all elements related to sustainable development, as well as public well-being. Essentially, this means consolidating the knowledge system into an efficient system for practical implementation. Reproducing the best practices in this regard is a way of boosting economic competitiveness and eliminating many of the negative factors associated with the burning of fossil fuels. The burning and transportation of biofuels not only causes air pollution in cities but also the deterioration of forests, although forests are supposedly being replanted.

The knowledge of the organisations in a municipality is not composed of individual elements, but of their entity. A comparative analysis of different countries reveals essential directions for improvement in Lithuania. First and foremost, a municipal policy can have a positive impact on the implementation of state responsibilities defined by the EU and Lithuanian legal bases. In the last decade, increasing policy requirements in the EU have influenced public policy in various fields. The development of RES and energy efficiency are no exception.

Current binding obligations for the Member States are contained in the Directive 2009/28 / EU of the European Parliament and the Council on the promotion of the use of energy from renewable sources (European Commission 2009) and Directive 2010/75/EU on industrial emissions (European Commission 2010). Lithuania has done a great deal of legal work transposing directives into national jurisdiction. The national RES development strategy and implementation plan have been prepared. After long discussions, the Law on Renewable Energy of the Republic of Lithuania of 2011 has also been adopted.

Member States have a choice as to how to allocate the responsibility for the implementation of national directives. Particular attention has been paid to the implementation strategies and finally, it was realised that from a territorial point of view, it would be most appropriate to implement RES plans on a larger scale. The Energy Efficiency Directive 2012/27/EU has already highlighted the potential role of self-government in promoting energy efficiency, stating that the Member States should encourage municipalities and other public organisations to adopt integrated sustainable energy efficiency plans with clear objectives, involving citizens in the preparation and implementation of these plans, and keeping them properly informed of the content, as well as the progress towards the objectives. Such plans can generate significant energy savings, especially if they are implemented through energy management systems that enable relevant public organisations to better manage their energy consumption. Exchanges of experience involving more innovative measures by cities, towns and other public organisations should be encouraged (European Commission 2012).

Only an organised body of knowledge allows the documents of these programmes to be transformed into the massive uptake of RES. A particular example is Denmark's economic policy. A key element is its strategic ambition to reach 100% of its energy supply from RES by 2050. Consequently, all RES and energy-saving measures find their niche in the overall development of energetics. In Denmark, tax policy, which is a key economic element, is characterised by high energy taxes on fossil fuel energy. This allows a level playing field between fossil fuel and RES technologies by eliminating external costs that are not evaluated in fossil fuel accounting. The optimal use of infrastructure, e.g. of DH systems, allows the large-scale utilisation of RES technologies.

The system of preconditions for the support of RES technologies in Lithuania is mainly involved with the realisation of short-term goals (by 2020, coinciding with the Structural Funds programme period), which blocks the diversification of fuel utilisation and diverts funds to, essentially, one type of fuel—biomass (wood and wood waste)—and prevents the implementation of solar, wind and geothermal energy.

Summarising the data in this section, it can be stated that municipalities, as non-profit organisations, have the potential to significantly influence the diversification and adoption of RES technologies on a much larger scale. On the other hand, much greater dissemination of knowledge is needed to describe not only the usefulness but also the potential negative effects of

RES technologies. Countries that have reached a high level of civilisation are a good example of how ecological balance and biodiversity can be achieved by combining various RES technologies, utilising existing DH infrastructure and, in particular, developing smart technologies that can also transform consumers into energy producers.

Now that ecological problems are becoming so evident, for the first time in human history, there has been a need to initiate and sign an agreement—the Paris Climate Change Agreement—which legally binds all parties and recognises that the replacement of fossil fuels with RES is a fundamental prerequisite for its implementation. The EU ratified the Paris Agreement in October 2016. It confirms the current economic theory, which is becoming increasingly widespread and whose vital importance is intuitively felt by people who regard nature as the basis of their lives, contrary to the way business values nature as a storehouse of raw materials.

This is the so-called circular economy, which is based on non-waste or naturally biodegradable waste technologies, particularly, the use of RES. The concept of the circular economy process is the exploitation of local resources and the application of waste technology to enable each region to create a specific environment for the exploitation of these resources, and to shape the local industry and agriculture, taking into account the true ecological and social value of such economic developments. The goal of nature, as well as the preservation of historical and cultural values, have found resonance and affirmation in the concept of sustainable economic development and most of the new ideas of the 21st century, in consideration of the future way of life. Practically, these ideas have begun to appear in the global ecological settlement movement. This movement is an initiative started by local organisations and group leaders whose main goal is to live in a clean, green environment, fostering community and social values, and promoting the development of a green economy. According to the international eco-community network, there are currently around 40,000 ecological settlements in 40 countries worldwide. Experience shows that this movement solves the problems of employment in rural and suburban areas, as well as helps with the promotion of business, the reduction of social exclusion, and the creation of alternative business ideas. Special attention is paid to the use of RES in these communities. At the same time, large-scale, long-term programmes currently exist worldwide, especially in Europe, aimed at ensuring that cities and regions are supplied solely with RES.

Such activities have been happening for quite some time, not just in terms of declarations. It might seem to require billions of dollars, but the circular economy theory and the supporting evidence show that more support and funds are needed in the start-up phase, especially in the development of information systems. After the initial stage, it becomes a normal business, except for the fact that respect for nature is rarely seen as an absolute value in business relationships. Educational activities are needed to show that the link between human activity and the eternal laws of natural evolution is broken. Cities and smaller rural or suburban communities play an especially important role in this process. During the long transformation process, there are two alternatives—either the further destruction of the natural environment or the emergence of an economy that operates based on the principles of the circular economy outlined above.

These extremely ambitious initiatives pale into insignificance compared to Denmark's and Germany's intent to ensure a 100 per cent supply of energy from RES by 2050. However, this requires extremely intensive educational and organisational activities of the city authorities, synchronising the realisation of the state goals, the funds and incentive mechanisms with the real possibilities in the cities and the proper regulatory framework.

With an organised knowledge system, municipal employees have effective means of solving energy problems, improving the ecological situation, creating jobs, optimising transport flows and implementing other social welfare goals with the same RES funding.

However, this requires the consolidation of various types of knowledge by linking it to the overall continuous knowledge structure of the organisation. One of the major challenges is to compare and highlight the tools and financial mechanisms that will be used in international practice in the future. However, the problem is much more serious than that. It is not enough to simply compare different instruments; it is also necessary to investigate the sources from which these instruments are financed. The widespread use of RES technologies in a systematic and targeted programmatic way, rather than in a chaotic way, requires a common policy in which territorial entities (cities, towns, communities) have a particular role to play (Klevas 2015).

An analysis of the laws currently in force in the Republic of Lithuania shows that they regulate municipal responsibilities in the field of RES development in considerable detail. The main problem, however, is that separate programmes, which do not have a consolidating commonality, are being developed for the implementation of individual EU directives. Most municipalities are delaying the implementation of statutory programmes and plans. The scarce funds available to municipalities are scattered.

It is not only necessary to anticipate the results of the utilisation of RES, but also to create the most appropriate assumptions and financial resources, which, if invested, would be able to achieve positive external effects.

However, when considering the possibility of including resource efficiency and RES in municipal planning documents, the question of funding arises. The implementation of autonomous municipal functions, including programming documents, is financed from the municipal budgets. These funds are limited, and it is difficult to expect the decisions to allocate funds to these areas on a larger scale. The functions delegated to the municipalities by the state are allocated from the state budget or state monetary funds and transferred to the municipalities as a special targeted grant. In any case, financial resources are very modest and scattered across individual programmes, so the central role of city government is organisational, enabling it to mobilise more resources. The main problem is the lack of specialists capable of developing integrated programmes in the energetics sector.

Therefore, the most important prerequisite for financing could be a public-private partnership (PPP), a long-term partnership agreement between a public sector body and a private sector representative in the implementation of a complex set of activities (such as infrastructure design, construction, reconstruction, repairs and maintenance). However, I believe that this notion needs to be extended to the rationale for financing sustainable urban development programmes by consolidating and managing funds on this basis. Examples of different forms of regional and even global partnerships can be used in the financing of the RES sector. They play an important role in financing the RES sector in developing countries (see Fig. 5-2).

This diagram shows how cities can form consolidated funds based on public-private partnerships. This requires essential conditions: the development of urban information systems and the integration of statutory programmes into a long-term, integrated programme for sustainable urban development that synchronises and does not duplicate short-term plans. Essentially, environmental programmes in all countries worldwide rely on the increased use of RES, and specific plans for DH would be the most rational means of integrating various RES projects into a single system, both on the production and the consumers' side.

The main advantage of RES projects is the combination of public and private efforts. The financial support provided by the partnership enables developing countries to transition more easily and rapidly to a new structure and economics—from a fossil fuel-based economy to an economy that meets the needs of consumers through clean resources.

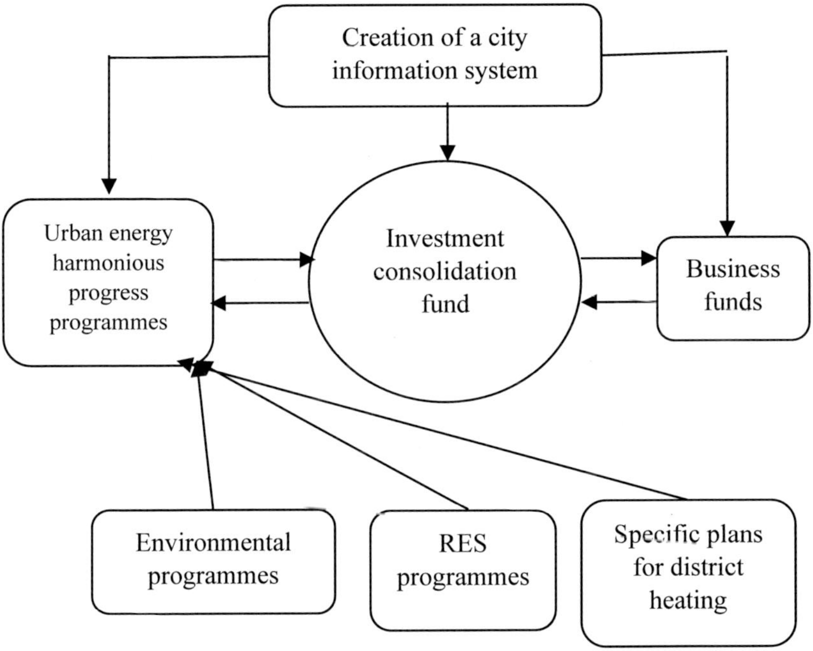

Fig. 5-2. A systematised way of financing opportunities in Lithuanian cities to support RES

The review of Eitan et al. (2019) brings to the fore the fast-growing and significant phenomenon of community and private sector renewable energy partnerships, which constitute a fundamental building block of the global renewable energy transformation.

> This review theorises on this issue by identifying six archetypes of the local community–private sector renewable energy partnerships, namely knowledge sharing, private finance, local consumption, land seeking, community employment, and lease archetypes. These archetypes are discussed with relation to key variables influencing partnership formation and perpetuation as part of the wider discussion regarding renewable energy partnerships between local communities and the private sector and the role they play in the energy transition to a low-carbon society (Eitan et al. 2019).

Advantages of Public-Private Partnerships:

- ensuring timely provision of higher quality public services
- distributing the risk of the project among the partners, according to their risk management capacity
- ensuring the necessary investment in the public sector
- in most cases, projects are timely and do not require unforeseen additional public spending
- enabling the private sector to secure long-term income
- using the skills and experience of the private sector in project implementation
- reducing the cost of managing risks through proper risk-sharing.

Of course, there might be disadvantages: the infrastructure or services created can be more expensive than expected, and postponing the public sector payments related to the partnership project may have a negative impact on the fiscal performance of the public sector in the following term.

CHAPTER TWO

THE BASICS OF GREEN SETTLEMENTS AND THE CIRCULAR ECONOMY MOVEMENT

Theoretical assumptions

When examining the concept of sustainable development and applying its ideas in practice, it has been observed that certain transformations are necessary for the concept of sustainable development itself, supplemented by rational, public wisdom. Modern, rapidly evolving information technologies make it possible to form practical scenarios that organically link technological advances to the needs of human societal development. However, it is becoming increasingly clear that it is human perception that is changing as technological advances far outweigh human attitudes and the desire to "defeat nature". Sustainable development has become the challenge of our times in all spheres of activity, including the economic, social and ecological environment. The issue of the energy security of future generations while preserving the natural environment is of particular importance. Various solutions are being explored and new concepts and theories are being developed in search of balance and ways of bringing humanity and nature closer together, and of how to reconnect with nature. Recently, the concept of the circular economy has become increasingly prominent, with the fundamental claim that sustainability in society requires a holistic approach to the production system, which must operate in a manner similar to that of the Earth's ecosystem. In it, plants produce oxygen and other substances needed by animals, and animals produce carbon dioxide and waste necessary for plants. For the system to function in nature (the ecosystem), it requires energy, which, in nature, comes mainly from the sun. In the society in which we live today, energy is currently derived mainly from the depths of the earth. An important element in an artificial material flow system is the decomposer, which could decompose waste into useful components, creating a closed material cycle and making the cycle non-waste (Juknys 2005). To balance the flows in the artificial environment, cycles in the anthroposphere must be close to the ecosystem cycles in their operating principles.

In the scientific literature, the sustainable development of economics is increasingly associated with concepts of green capital, while the new concept of economic development is associated with the introduction of new criteria that give meaning to the interaction between man and nature. Economist T. Jackson (2009), in his book "Prosperity without Growth", states that prosperity and a better quality of life are possible in another economic space, where the main driving force is not only value-added capital but also communities and their social capital. In the new green capital economy, prosperity will be created through smart management methods and the ideas of the sustainable development concept". The essence of green capitalism is discussed in the scholarly articles of Henderson (2006) and D. H. Meadows, D. L. Meadows and J. Randers (1992). Interpretation of the sustainable development concept employing "green" environmental indicators is the subject of research by authors such as Rees (2000), M. Wackernagel (1999) and others.

Recently, an approach viewing development without absolute growth or materiality has evolved, focusing on development based on social principles. Concentration on economic growth is often a form of justification in terms of the devastation of nature. Jean-Jacques Rousseau, in the 18th century, warned that man should start thinking about the direction of civilisation's evolution, about the nature and meaning of his lifestyle. His slogan of "returning to nature" is not, however, a revival of a primitive lifestyle. On the contrary, it is an evolution of the human community based on the application of the latest technologies, avoiding competition with everyone and abandoning the desire to "defeat nature".

This concept is explored in the scientific papers of Rifkin (2012), Jackson (2009), Wackernagel (2002), Moran et al. (2009), (Kitzes (2009), and Robe (2002).

The interrelationships of indicators over the past decade have been addressed through the analysis of economic growth, sustainable development and the ecological aspects that link them, i.e. the ability of the ecosystem to recover, ecological capacity, or "load-carrying". Ecosystem services and resource depletion are studied in the works of researchers such as Rees (2000), Wackernagel (2002) and others.

Čiegis (2009), Paulauskas (1999) and others have written in detail about sustainable development and the impact of state interventionism on sustainable economic development in Lithuania.

Circular economy principles—the theoretical basis for green settlements

In the field of sustainable economic theory, the concept of the circular economy emerges from the sustainable development concept.

> While the terms Circular Economy and sustainability are increasingly gaining traction with academia, industry, and policymakers, the similarities and differences between both concepts remain ambiguous. The relationship between the concepts is not made explicit in the literature, which is blurring their conceptual contours and constrains the efficacy of using the approaches in research and practice (Geissdoerfer et al. 2017).

Their research focuses on the never-ending cycle of the production of products and energy, where virtually no waste is produced, and all the resulting waste is recycled. An important aspect of the circular economy cycle is the systematic approach which requires a detailed analysis of the amounts and flows of resources and energy, in order to manage and control the distribution of energy, reduce waste or convert it into useful substances. This relates to the territorial dimension of the development. The development of the region's energy economy, in accordance with the principles of the circular economy, using as many local and RES as possible, is analysed by M. S. Andersen (2006). But even more important is the fact that different theoretical approaches must go through a "laboratory" test and the possibility of synthesising different concepts. Although the circular economy is no longer a new idea, lately, the sustainable consumption model has been receiving attention and creating the potential for a "greener" future (Dar, Lin and Chen 2015) and (Bartl 2015).

> The circular economy enables not only the efficient use of resources but also economic growth. In order to maintain the value of products, materials and resources in the economy for as long as possible, waste generation is significantly reduced. Today we see the enormous environmental impact of the linear economy and the extremely harmful patterns of our daily consumption that make the transition to a circular economy inevitable (Rakštytė-Hoimian 2019).

Over the past nine years, Lithuania's openness to eco-innovation has started to grow alongside the business investment in non-technological innovation. Since 2010, Lithuania has moved from 23rd to 16th place in the eco-innovation index, published by the European Commission—today it outperforms neighbouring Latvia and Poland. The index compares the

Member States, according to 16 different indicators, grouped into five categories: eco-innovation cost, eco-innovation activity, eco-innovation performance, national resource efficiency and socio-economic impact. Out of these five areas, Lithuania is the most successful in ensuring the positive socio-economic impact of eco-innovation—even above the EU average. However, we should make great efforts when investing in this area. As far as the implementation of the circular economy is concerned, Lithuania's progress is insufficient. Although the idea of a circular economy is spreading, neither the public nor private sectors are fully prepared. There is a definite lack of tax incentives for the circular economy products or services. The recycling rate is one of the lowest in the EU, at just 7% of the total amount of waste. There is no clear policy and strategy for promoting eco-innovation and recycling. However, in recent years, businesses and NGOs have been focusing on initiatives to support recycling and the reuse of products. From 2016 to 2017, areas of recycling and efficient waste management were the subject of tremendous technological development, which has given impetus to the concept of the circular economy becoming increasingly embedded in public discourse. The concept of the circular economy is being extended not only to industry and business but to the population as well. Consumers are encouraged not only to rethink their daily consumption habits but also to find ways to use the product for secondary or tertiary purposes. It is no secret—it often requires not only creativity and will, but also time.

The renewed EU industrial policy strategy pays particular attention to the role of the circular economy and sees the transition to a circular economy as one of the fundamental ways of implementing the 2030 Sustainable Development Strategy. Germany is showing great results and progress in mastering the principles of the circular economy. According to the daily political newspaper "Politico", its economy is the most circular of all EU Member States. This is due to the high level of innovation in the circular economy sectors and a reliable and well-developed waste recycling system. The high level of "circularity" is also due to the fact that the German economy, being one of the largest economies in the EU, is able to attract more private investment and create more jobs related to the circular economy. Last year, the circular economy sectors in Germany attracted $28.7 million investment. Meanwhile, in other countries with similar economic levels (per capita GDP)—the Netherlands, Sweden or Denmark—it was 2-5 million euros. In Lithuania, 0.4 million euros is invested in these sectors of the economy. Another noteworthy example is the Czech Republic. Compared to most countries in Western and Northern Europe, it is capable of producing the least waste per capita. There is 339 kg of municipal waste and 81 kg of food waste per capita per year. In comparison, in the Netherlands, there is over 500 kg per capita of both types of waste each year. In Lithuania, the situation regarding the generation of food waste is not critical (119 kg per capita per year), but one should pay attention to municipal waste, the size per capita of which is as high as 444 kg. The circular economy, public procurement and the transition to a circular economy are not limited to certain materials or sectors. It is a systemic change, affecting the whole economy and covering all products and services. According to Justė Rakštytė-Hoimian, a consultant at the Lithuanian Innovation Centre:

> Governments with the power to promote business and products based on the circular economy could be the main drivers of this systemic change. One way to create these incentives is through public procurement. Public authorities can choose to buy green goods, services or jobs and thus promote and support green innovation and the transition to a circular economy.

The EU Circular Economy Action Plan identifies public procurement as one of the most important tools for achieving the circular economy objectives. Public procurement accounts for as much as 20% of EU GDP and, with its large share of the European consumption pyramid, plays an important role in the transition to a circular economy. The European Commission encourages national governments to improve their national public procurement systems, not only by focusing on green criteria but also by basing them on the principles of the circular economy. Even though the Lithuanian public sector supports public procurement, encouraging environmental initiatives, circular economy initiatives (including circular public procurement) are only promoted latently. Finally, Lithuanian law and the legislative system do not even have a separate definition of circular procurement. On the other hand, there are no restrictions on this type of procurement either. The latest edition of the Law on Public Procurement contains several articles creating favourable conditions for the implementation of circular procurement in Lithuania. Thus, the drive to move towards a greener future through public procurement only lacks political will.

In China, evaluation of the effectiveness of the circular economy in regard to environmental protection and economic aspects is a very popular area of study. Also, an extremely important aspect is the creation of systematic criteria in terms of the circular economy (Geng, Fu, Sarkis and Xue 2011).

The idea of creating and developing green settlements was formed on this exact theoretical basis. A "green" or ecological settlement is primarily concerned with understanding the laws of ecological evolution and with a holistic approach to shaping ecological lifestyles. In nature, living organisms and the interactions between their environments are interrelated processes that work together to sustain life and ensure the purposefulness of the system (Palojarvi 2013). Therefore, the development of the green settlement model is primarily aimed at preserving the integrity of nature and emphasising the dependent position of each part, including man (Kalenda 2007).

Organisational principles and the implementation experience of green settlements

The technology of power generation from RES, which is the basis for the development of the "green" settlement's energy economy, arose 40 years ago. At the same time, the methodology for justifying RES promotion measures has emerged, enabling the assessment and enhancement of the efficiency and competitiveness of RES technologies. In order to understand the circumstances in which the RES market is efficient, and in which the RES market is failing to produce effective results, the researchers analysed market failures that prevent the development of RES technology to the required extent.

The uptake of RES and the practical application of RES technologies are associated with a wide variety of resources, raw materials, technologies, and manufactured products. Therefore, the optimal choice of technology for the utilisation of primary resources and transformation of raw materials into suitable products and forms of energy is a complex task, where the search for solutions is carried out using optimisation methods. As a green settlement is a living laboratory for eco-innovation and sustainable development solutions in the fields of construction engineering, energy use, waste and wastewater management, transport use, agricultural and food production, and consumer culture (Palojarvi 2013), it is best to use systematic methods of analysis of sustainable development to carry out the research in such a "laboratory", which helps to understand the current situation, predict potential solutions and evaluate the consequences of the decisions made.

Materials and products of traditionally developed conventional settlements which use fossil fuels generate the waste which leads to environmental pollution. Meanwhile, in theory, green settlement economies replicate natural processes, which are an ideal example of waste-free technology. The amount of waste generated in the energy sector can be reduced by increasing the efficiency of primary energy sources which promote the use of RES, and by choosing environmentally friendly products and equipment made of components that are less harmful to the environment. As the energy economy develops in accordance with circular economy and bioregional principles, the environmental impact can be reduced by more efficient use of RES, the use of which in the region can create a unique environment for the exploitation of these resources (Bireckland 2008). However, the amount of resource depletion cannot exceed nature's ability to restore these resources, or these renewable resources must be treated as non-renewable (Čiegis 2009). A comprehensive analysis of RES resources, energy supply and demand assessment can help to improve the management and control of energy flows in the region, reducing waste and converting it into useful materials. The development of the energy economics of the regional territorial unit, according to the principles of the circular economy, encourages the use of a wider range of local and RES. Balancing the energy flows in the region is associated with the widest possible use of local and renewable sources. The idea of "green" settlements in Western European countries is an attempt to address a number of related issues, including the problem of energy supply. However, finding the right solutions using the criteria of sustainable development does not always produce quick and effective results. Proponents of the theory of sustainable development argue that sustainable development must be supplemented with one additional component—the knowledge-based economy. In this context, green settlements should become a new economic force in which civil society builds social and intellectual capital (Rifkin 2012).

Implementing the principles of green settlements involves a change in people's habits and mentality, which is a complex and lengthy process. In addition, this is reliant on system-wide changes, so these processes cannot be executed quickly. It is important not to deviate from the essence of the concept of sustainable development, which is the principle that current developments must meet our needs without compromising the ability of future generations to meet their own needs.

The Habitat II Declaration states that cities and settlements are the incubators of civilisation and the engines of growth that accelerate the evolution of knowledge, culture and traditions, as well as industry and commerce. The Declaration also emphasises that properly designed and managed urban settlements create favourable prospects for human development and protection of the world's natural resources.

Gradually, groups of people began to realise that the best way to reverse the current trend was to start changing their lifestyles. Such initiatives have formed a movement of green communities that have united groups of people into eco, or green settlements. These communities were formed on a bottom-up basis, mostly in sparsely populated areas, homesteads or villages.

The prototype of green settlements is the eco-village, officially recognised by the United Nations for the first time in 1998. An organic settlement is a small community of several hundred people who seek to demonstrate via their lifestyles that living in harmony with nature is not only possible but also healthy and meaningful. In such a community, human relationships and social culture are associated with a "new" culture of communication, where people help each other, share things, and solve problems together without any financial gains. One of the basic ideas of the community is that economic activities (food production, construction, energy production, waste management, etc.) must not harm the environment. An ecological settlement is a harmonious settlement with a balance between natural cycles and human activity. In terms of meeting its energy needs, an eco-friendly settlement is a "green" settlement that aims to use local and RES.

Ecological settlements have also formed in urban areas as small districts and groups of houses using the characteristics of the living environment, i.e. the homes are constructed of natural and environmentally friendly materials, using RES and designed as per the following eco-friendly principles:

- Community
- Reducing consumption
- Strengthening of spiritual and cultural identity
- Reducing mobility
- Waste management, waste-free technology
- Use of indigenous and RES.

When considering the development of green settlements, the following types should be distinguished:

1. "Green" or eco-communities are groups of people consisting of several families or a larger group of several hundred people, who are united in a community with the common goal of creating a living space (in a new or existing, but sparsely populated area), sharing an eco-friendly point of view and ideas about life, fostering organic farming and organic economy, using RES, reducing consumption and mobility, and strengthening spiritual capital and cultural identity.
2. Eco-villages are residential areas of several to several hundred hectares in which several houses (single-family houses) or groups of houses may be located, forming an image of a rural area where eco-communities cherish ecological traditions of living.

3. "Green" settlements are groups of eco-villages in which the eco-community strives to ensure that social life and economic activities are conducted in accordance with the principles of green living. In most cases, all residents of such settlements are subject to the same eco-friendly rules that must be observed by all people living and operating there, which have defined areas of activity and directions.

4. "Green urban areas" are areas of settlements or cities in which the natural environment is maintained (or restored) and human activities do not disturb the natural way of life.

5. "Green cities" are populated areas (usually existing cities, but may include new cities), in which human economic activity interacts with the processes of the ecosystem in a coherent way. "Green cities" are a combination of several or dozens of "green areas" that have the infrastructure of regular cities, but where activities are balanced according to ecosystem cycles.

Residential areas are created by promoting the management of the city, the settlement or a part of it by institutional and political means, therefore, it is considered that the form and construction of urban society is not the most important aspect—it is the form of urban organisation and management. The green settlement seeks sustainability through various land use, environmental, institutional, social, technological and economic policies. An ecological settlement can be a new or existing settlement, as well as a part of the city (district), a village or even a few homesteads, where the aim is to create ecological living conditions that follow the principles of sustainable development.

The present-day green settlement is based on the concept of sustainable development, applying information and communication technologies and taking into account cultural, aesthetic and ethnic criteria, creating a place where traditions and spirituality are in tune with progress and technology. The concept of the green settlement is based on economic and technological criteria, taking into account cultural, ecological and spiritual aspects.

Green settlements cannot be created in an empty space isolated from the infrastructure necessary for living. They are developing in the context of existing infrastructure; therefore, it is essential to expect a long-term transformation process. Achieving the objective of producing a major share of energy from renewable sources can only be achieved in stages, as well as in a structured and clear way. In addition, there is a need to develop the waste management system and ensure the recycling of biodegradable organic waste, using digestion, fermentation and biogas recycling technologies to promote the diversification of fuels. Depending on current geographical and natural conditions, modern technology can produce 20-

80% (in rare cases 100%) of the energy required in a given region. By combining all of these energy-saving, efficiency and production methods, it is possible to achieve all energy production without the use of fossil fuels. Such energy development requires not only financial and human resources but also political decisions and willingness. At the time, the prospects for new energy sources have not been sufficiently explored, and the use of green energy also does not always meet consumers' expectations, therefore, the use of renewable energy and renewable technologies should be a major priority in terms of sustainable development in the energy economy.

Taking into account natural resources, environmental degradation and environmental damage, the entire production process or the life cycle of the product—from the extraction of the resources needed to produce the product, to the final consumption (utilisation)—is assessed. It is necessary to transform our production methods, consumption habits and communication skills to create a sustainable living environment so that the activities do not disrupt the orderly development of the ecosystem.

Chapter Three

Addressing Forest Conservation Issues

Lithuanian scientist, J. Brėdikis, once a proponent of technological trends in medicine, has recently demonstrated in his works how to evaluate the interaction between technology and Nature. I will quote a few thoughts that stood out to me:

> Human invasion of nature is always risky. Due to the enormous demand for wood, forests are being cut down recklessly. With the disappearance of forests, wastelands are being formed—as a result, the vital energy of natural life is rapidly declining. Trees are the Chinese acupuncture needles, tucked into the ground. At their roots, they come in contact with the energy of the earth, and at their tops, like antennas, with the higher energies of the biosphere. We sought to control Nature, not as hosts, but as pests against nature. It can be said that we have created a program for the destruction of nature (Brėdikis 2015).

One of the most important questions today is the protection and expansion of our forests. In this context, it would be banal to talk about the powerful CO_2 absorbent properties of the forests, which they have naturally, as well as the ability to protect and provide a safe shelter for various forms of life. It is truly terrible to even talk about a widespread axiom, stating that burning wood is a CO_2 neutral act, considering that the wood has absorbed enough CO_2 throughout its lifetime to make the act of burning it and, therefore, influencing climate change, completely rational and justifiable. In other words, wood deserves to be burnt because of its merits for nature. It is a terrible idea when you actually look into it.

In 2018, the daily Lithuanian newspaper "Lietuvos Rytas" publicised an article (Lietuvos Rytas 2018): "Scientists break the myth of biofuels and say that the EU can make a fatal mistake". I will cite the most important thoughts of this article.

On 17 January 2018, The EP voted to strengthen the EU renewable energy targets. However, the EP decision did not include an amendment proposing to reduce the production and use of biofuels. This change was particularly supported by many NGOs. After the launch of this resolution, a study published in the journal, Environmental Research Letters, declared that bioenergy sources, such as wood, could be more harmful than coal, in the short term. Although bioenergy production from wood can reduce long-term CO_2 concentrations compared to fossil fuels, the use of biofuels initially increases CO_2 levels and thus exacerbates climate change in the short term—up to the year 2100. Even if we counted on wood to replace all carbon, the most polluting fuel, it would still make things worse, stated researchers from the Massachusetts Institute of Technology (MIT), Climate Interactive, University of Massachusetts (UMass), Lowell Climate Change Initiative and UMass Experts from the Lowell Department of Environmental, Earth and Atmospheric Sciences. According to the authors, with the EU's insistence on "carbon-neutral biofuels", it is wrong to think that reforestation can adequately compensate for CO_2 emissions due to biofuel production and combustion. The assumption of neutrality is not appropriate because it does not take into account the short-term—decades-to-century—increase in CO_2 in the atmosphere due to the use of biofuels, experts state in their findings. As the EU is the third-largest CO_2 emitter in the world, after China and the US, such a mistaken approach to biofuels could be fatal in reducing CO_2 and implementing the Paris Agreement. Short-term increases in CO_2 emissions from biofuels could undermine current EU targets to reduce greenhouse gas emissions by at least 40%, compared to 1990 levels, by 2030. By claiming that biofuels are CO_2 neutral—as the EU, the UK and other countries do—we are wrong to believe that reforestation quickly and completely outweighs the emissions from the production and burning of biofuels". A land-use specialist of the Berlin-based Mercator Research Institute for Global Commons and Climate Change has also noticed this shortcoming. This is a conceptual error that runs counter to climate change mitigation goals in Europe's renewable energy plans. However, the EU decision has not yet been implemented.

The special importance of the forests and the scientific analysis were provided by a large body of different organisations. I will share the most important conclusion of the article prepared by approximately 20 people, representing 15 organisations, on the strategic importance of forests in terms of planet preservation:

> Forest-driven water and energy cycles are poorly integrated into regional, national, continental and global decision-making on climate change adaptation, mitigation, land use and water management. This constrains humanity's ability to protect our planet's climate and life-sustaining functions. Forests and trees must be recognized as prime regulators within the water, energy and carbon cycles. If these functions are ignored, planners will be unable to assess, adapt to or mitigate the impacts of changing land

> cover and climate. Our call to action targets a reversal of paradigms, from a carbon-centric model to one that treats the hydrologic and climate-cooling effects of trees and forests as the first order of priority (Elisson et al. 2017).

Forests are one of the main natural assets of Lithuania, serving the well-being of the state and its citizens, protecting the stability of the landscape and the quality of the environment. Regardless of the form of forest ownership, forests are first and foremost a national asset that must be preserved for future generations, meeting the ecological, economic and social needs of society.

> The global functions of forests are: to absorb most of the sun's radiation; to produce and maintain, for the most part, photosynthetic biological growth and thus biomass; to maintain and regulate carbon, nitrogen and oxygen circulation, to maintain and regulate water circulation between the atmosphere, the earth's surface, plants and atmosphere (again); to accumulate rainfall on the surface of the earth and thus slow down the runoff water; influencing and levelling the temperature, precipitation, air humidity in the region; supplying wood (Beirsh, Borneo and Brunner 1998).

Lithuanian forests are rich in flora and fauna, but their increasing use threatens this diversity. Most of the forests in Lithuania are no longer natural, they are shaped to meet human needs—to grow as much high-quality raw materials for the industry as possible. Some species from the oldest forests have been able to survive in the landscape of farm forests, but other species of plants, animals and fungi have disappeared, or their numbers have declined significantly. Currently, almost 300 species of forest organisms are listed in the Lithuanian Red Book. Nearly 200 protected species are threatened by deforestation. For 39 species of the Red Book, deforestation might have a positive impact, 27 species of which only favour selective deforestation, while complete clearing of the forest is disastrous for them. Thus, deforestation negatively affects 27% of endangered species included in the Red Book in Lithuania, while at least 5% of all species included in the Lithuanian Red Book may feel a positive impact. One of the most brutal forms of destruction of nature is the clear-cutting of the forests. It destroys the entire forest ecosystem—from flora and fauna to the soil. All symbiotic relationships that are of special importance to the restoration of the forest are cut off. After clearing a forest, it is impossible to restore it to its pre-felling state. In Lithuania, the forest of long-lived trees is the last stage of succession, but after the destruction of the entire ecosystem, in the case of clear felling, all stages of the succession have to pass again to get the forest back to its pre-felling state. In natural conditions, the forest of long-lived trees regenerates after a clear cut, not even in a hundred years, but over a much longer period. “The most important factors of clear-cutting are the direct destruction of species, the destruction of their habitat and the integrity of the forest itself” (Beirsh, Borneo and Brunner 1998).

Even though forest trees are affected by climate change in many ways, they are the natural “lungs” of the earth that help to absorb carbon dioxide—one of the main causes of climate warming. Absorption of CO_2 in the forest occurs through photosynthesis, whereby plants (trees, shrubs and herbaceous plants) synthesise organic carbon compounds (glucose), which are stored in living plant biomass—leaves/needles, trunks/stems, roots. As the tree grows, more and more carbon is “bound” in the organic compounds of the wood’s biomass, and oxygen is “liberated” and returned to the atmosphere. Wood not only supplies us with oxygen during photosynthesis but also absorbs and stores atmospheric carbon (which is in the form of CO_2 in the atmosphere) as a building material for wood. As it is explained in the comment from the State Forest Service, the annual CO_2 absorption is directly proportional to the volume growth of the wood. The utility of renewables, which differs from oil and gas in its ability to ensure energy security for future generations, is not systematically evaluated in economics. Finally, the usefulness of different types of RES also varies. And this is one of the main highlights of the concept of sustainable energy development.

In the theoretical context, the main goal is to develop a scientifically based systematic approach for motivating the use of RES. One of the key roles of science is to provide information to improve the shaping of the development policy in the decision-making process. This requires a substantial improvement in scientific understanding, long-term research-based assessment, and raising the country’s scientific competence. A research scheme is necessary that would provide answers to questions that remain unclear when RES promotion measures are transferred from international practice without taking sufficient account of the situation of the national economy into the evolutionary process of societal development.

CONCLUSION

The essence of the paradigm is the totality of assumptions, concepts, values and activities that reflect the worldview and perception of reality in a given community.

The basic paradigm that has dominated for several centuries regarding the interaction between the economic activity of humanity and Nature remains unchanged. In this paradigm, Nature is considered to be an inexhaustible source of physical resources and an infinite absorber of by-products of the production processes. It is believed that environmental damage will always be repaired if necessary. What is worse is that the concept of progress is identified with the pursuit of economic progress, while the individual and his life goals remain within the frame of *homo economicus*. And this is undoubtedly a major obstacle to progress.

The paradigm of harmonious progress is based on a worldview which, defining it in short, recognises Nature, including the laws which govern man, as the determining power for humanity's existence. I refer to the great humanists who created the philosophy of the meaning of human life and its purpose, which views Nature as the basis of human being and existence. Economic progress is closely linked to great respect for Nature as an intrinsic value, not just an inexhaustible wealth of resources that can be recklessly exploited. Harmonious progress is a form of economic and social evolution that meets the needs of the present without compromising future generations. When talking about future generations, it is not just human beings, but all kinds of life, relying on land, water, and natural resources for their existence. The forest acts as a defensive bastion, transforming the exhaled and produced CO_2 into fresh air.

The concept of sustainable energy development is based on an old paradigm. Without a basic paradigmatic approach to nature conservation, the relentless pursuit of economic growth beyond natural boundaries will not help to achieve the goals of sustainable development. Sustainable development remains a slogan without real content. Therefore, the concept of sustainable development needs to be fundamentally replaced by the concept and content of the paradigm of harmonious progress in nature conservation and regeneration.

The most important problem that forms the core of the solution to the problems of harmonious progress is that waste—including waste in the form of harmful emissions, causing climate change—is generated during the process of transforming (burning) fossil energy, especially in transport. Therefore, the most important emphasis in attempting to define the paradigm of harmonious advancement in energy is the breakdown of energy resources into fossil fuels, produced over millions of years by natural evolution (e.g. coal, oil and natural gas) and RES (solar, wind and environmental, etc.), that do not pollute the environment.

The transformation of energy from exhaustive fossil fuels, causing enormous pollution, to RES is considered an expression of the progress of life in general, as this process no longer contradicts the fundamental laws of Nature, which seem to be disappearing from the horizon of human life due to the incredible advancement of technology. This means that a change in people's mentality is crucial for success, and the most important element in terms of energetics would be the understanding of the importance of RES. The cornerstone of the paradigm of harmonious progress in energy is the emphasis on the economic valuation of renewable energies.

The paradigm of harmonious progress differs from the one-sided conceptualisation of the technological progress and the pace of economic growth, in terms that it synthesises and summarises thoughts and knowledge that "reconcile" scientific and technological achievements with the eternal laws of nature's evolution that have been expressed by prominent authors long ago.

Energy markets cannot ensure all the important energy sustainability priorities themselves—security of energy supply, reduction of the environmental impact, and access to energy for poorer towns and villages, as well as the wider use of RES, and the ability for future generations to have available energy sources. Research into these and other issues have highlighted serious problems which arise when evaluating various aspects of sustainable development in terms of economic theory. The problem-solving necessities determine the research directions, although a unified methodological basis is required.

The increasing use of RES, the application of circular economy principles, smart grids, eco-cities and green settlements (communities) are the new signs of a rebirth, the emergence of which is a symbol of a new reverse direction in Nature, which could connect the technological progress with the human mission in Nature. The task of realising a paradigm of harmonious progress means combining the latest positive trends and theoretically developing these phenomena on a large scale. It is necessary to lay down guidelines for the transitional period based on the latest technological advancements, the purposeful application of the circular economy, and the mass ecological movements of people appalled by such apparent technical domination in art, science, and cultural life in general. During the long transformation process, there are two alternatives—either the further destruction of the natural environment or the emergence of an economy that operates based on the principles of the circular economy outlined above.

The issue of shifting to a more sustainable point of view will not solve itself without a change in the underlying paradigm, in other words, without emphasising the imperative of Nature's conservation. However, bearing in mind that solid biomass (wood and wood waste) currently plays a disproportionate role in the heating sector, since almost all future heat production is expected to be based on biomass, it is certain that the old paradigm-based strategy is still leading to a roadblock. Biomass is often misinterpreted as a renewable resource, even though it can only be viewed in a relatively CO_2-neutral way. In the meantime, it is sufficient to note that the great appreciation for the mass utilisation of biofuel is a clear path to destruction.

It is necessary to solve the underlying theoretical problems that are caused by the market economy's inability to avoid the disastrous effects of fossil fuel combustion on the environment, by ensuring the reliability of the energy supply and an adequate amount of energy resources for future generations. Extremely damaging stereotypes regarding allegedly contradictory support for renewable energy must be overcome by employing a thorough analysis of the environmental impact caused by different types of RES. The uniform interpretation of all RES technologies, despite their differences in various aspects, especially as regards their regeneration properties and their environmental impact, is even worse.

Economic theory explains the fundamental reason why there is a lack of demand for certain goods and services on the market (even though they are highly beneficial to society). The main reason is that the external benefits generated by the good or service are not reflected in the direct market operations and, thus, in the price. In the case of RES, this is a crucial moment. The external environmental benefits initiated by the use of RES could be the best example of external value. The use of RES reduces negative environmental effects, saves organic fuel resources and helps to assimilate new technologies. Demand for RES in the market does not reflect the previously mentioned public benefit caused by the use of energy made from renewable sources. The benefits are scattered among various users: individuals, future generations, cities, companies, etc. Even the people who do not participate in the transactions of this market can sometimes get a free share of benefits.

Capital-intensive reliability and assurance measures for energy provision would achieve a synergic effect if, in parallel, the commitments of the Climate Change Programme are addressed. Therefore, it is possible—and necessary—to combine different sources of funding on a unified basis. Essentially, the deployment of RES technologies solves many problems in cities and settlements, the localisation of which is extremely important from a territorial point of view.

As local government performs a number of functions in the energy sector, municipalities could play an important role in promoting assumptions regarding sustainable energy development. On the other hand, structures that could concentrate various financial resources, which are available at state level, are scarce in cities. These financial resources, together with private investments, would allow the development of renewable energy technologies on a significantly larger scale. Modern smart grids can already handle fluctuations in the electrical circuit almost ideally and respond immediately to cities' energy needs. This requires a broad and properly structured knowledge of the natural and social processes that lead to sustainable development and its evaluation.

The concept of the knowledge economy has strong links and interconnections with the concept of sustainable development. The concept of sustainable development arose when there was an obvious threat to nature caused by the enormous waste from the production process, which could no longer be denied. Clean air, which does not have a market price, is used by all of us for free—until now it has been largely free of environmental pollution as well. Nowadays, there is widespread talk about the structure of knowledge as a production factor that has an obvious value and even creates added value but has no market price, as it is essentially considered a public good. It currently means being educated by the public science and education system, although, in the open market, the price of science is still only indirectly measured, e.g., as brain drain losses.

The most important practical value of the methodology based on the knowledge economy is that it combines the two major programmes of this age—the Energy Strategy and the Climate Change Programme—into a single methodological framework. The methodology of energy development, besides the energy effect, simultaneously ensures the implementation of the defined climate change commitments—the synergies are achieved in terms of investments.

It should be noted that when comparing RES, they mainly differ in one essential respect. Solar, wind and geothermal energy represent the natural, infinite, eternal, non-generated regeneration phenomenon, the economic evaluation of which has to be based on economic regularity. This regularity denies one of the fundamental laws of the economy, which declares that as demand increases, the price of a commodity increases as well. This is true for virtually all fossil fuels and biomass. In contrast, it is the opposite for natural RES—the higher the demand, the more energy is produced, and the more the price of energy created using natural RES drops.

Meanwhile, biomass is a product of the economic activity that can only be partially described as renewable. At present, the most harmful is the short-sighted policy of promoting biofuels, which has given the green light to mass deforestation. Looking at the forest as a raw material for fuel production, tremendous damage can be caused to its natural biodiversity as well as to the whole of society. There is a definite lack of knowledge and research in this area—this is the main rationale for such a huge increase in demand for forest material portrayed as fuel.

The idea of creating and developing green settlements was formed on the theoretical basis of the circular economy. A "green" or ecological settlement is primarily concerned with understanding the laws of ecological evolution and with a holistic approach to shaping ecological lifestyles. In nature, living organisms and the interactions between their environment are interrelated processes that work together to sustain life and ensure the purposefulness of the system. Therefore, the development of the green settlement model is primarily aimed at preserving the integrity of nature and emphasising the dependent position of each part, including man. Implementing the principles of a green settlement involves a change in people's habits and mentality, which is a complex and lengthy process.

REFERENCES

Adamkus, V. 2016. *Interviews without protocol* (in Lithuanian). Vilnius: Versus Aureus.

Andersen, M. S. 2006. "An introductory note on the environmental economics of the circular economy". *Sustain. Sci.*, no. 2: 133-40. doi: 10.1007/s11625-006-0013-6.

Andersen, H., Barker, P., and Chen, X. 2003. "Thomas Kuhn and Cognitive Science". In *Thomas Kuhn,* edited by T. Nickles, 212-245. Cambridge: Cambridge University Press.

Arcos, A., V. A. Gomez, and E. F. G. Garcia. 2019. "Self-sufficient renewable energy supply in urban areas: Application to the city of Seville". *Sustainable Cities and Society* 46 (April). https://doi.org/10.1016/j.scs.2019.101450.

Asmelash, H. B. 2015. "Energy Subsidies and WTO Dispute Settlement: Why Only Renewable Energy Subsidies Are Challenged". *J Int Econ Law* 18: 261-85. doi: 10.1093/jiel/jgv024.

Atkočiūnienė, Z. O. 2008. *Impact of Knowledge Management on Sustainable Development* (in Lithuanian). Vilnius: Information Science.

Bayulken, B., and D. Huisingh. 2015. "Are lessons from eco-towns helping planners make more effective progress in transforming cities into sustainable urban systems: a literature review". (part 2 of 2). *J. Clean Prod.* doi: 10.1016/j.jclepro.2014.12.099.

Banister, D. 2008. "The sustainable mobility paradigm". *Transport* 15: 73-80.

Barbier, E. B. 1987. "The concept of sustainable economic development". *Environmental Conservation*, no. 14 (2): 101-110.

Barkauskas, V., and K. Barkauskienė. 2011. *Importance of the knowledge economy for intellectual capital formation* (in Lithuanian). Kaunas: Technologija.

Bartl, A. 2015. "Withdrawal of the circular economy package: A wasted opportunity or a new challenge?" *Waste Manag.*, no. 44:1-2. doi: 10.1016/j.wasman.2015.08.003.

Barton, H. 2000. *Sustainable Communities: The Potential for Eco-neighbourhoods*. London: Earthscan Publications.

Bauman, Z. 2015. *Culture in fluid modernity* (in Lithuanian). Vilnius: Apostrofa.

Bazaz, A., P. Bertoldi, M. Buckeridge, A. Cartwright, H. de Coninck, F. Engelbrecht, D. Jacob, et al. 2018. (December). *Summary for Urban Policymakers – What the IPCC Special Report on 1.5C Means for Cities*. Intergovernmental Panel on Climate Change (IPCC).

Beckerman, W. 1994. "Sustainable development: is it a useful concept?" *Environmental Values*, no. 3: 191-209.

Beirsh, U., U. Borneo, and H. Brunner. 1998. *Forests, their future* (in Lithuanian). Vilnius: Lithuanian dictionary.

Bergmann, A., S. Colombo, and N. Hanley. 2008. "Rural versus urban preferences for renewable energy developments". *Ecol. Econ*. 65: 616-25. doi: 10.1016/j.ecolecon.2007.08.011.

Bicknell, K. B., R. J. Ball, R. Cullen and H. R. Bigsby. 1998. "New methodology for the ecological footprint with an application to the New Zealand economy". *Ecological Economics* 27, no. 149: 60.

Birekland, J. 2008. *Positive development from vicious circles to virtuous cycles through built environment design*. London: Sterling VA.

Bloomberg. 2014. New Energy Finance, http://www.economist.com/news/21566414-alternative-energy-will-no-longer-be-alternative-sunny-uplands.

Bobinaite, V., and D. Tarvydas. 2014. "Financing instruments and channels for the increasing production and consumption of renewable energy: Lithuanian case". *Renew. Sustain. Energy Rev*. 38: 259-76. doi: 10.1016/j.rser.2014.05.039.

Boulding, K. E. 1991. "What Do We Want to Sustain? Environmentalism and Human Evaluations". In *Ecological Economics: Science and Management*, edited by R. Constanza. New York: Columbia University Press.

Braungart, M., W. McDonough, and A. Bollinger. 2006. "Cradle-to-cradle design: creating healthy emissions – a strategy for eco-effective product and system design". *J. Clean. Prod.,* no. 15: 1337-48. doi: 10.1016/j.jclepro.2006.08.003.

Brėdikis, J. 2015. *In a different glance* (in Lithuanian). Vilnius: Santara.

Broto, C., and H. Bulkeley. 2013. "A survey of urban climate change experiments in 100 cities". *Glob. Environ. Change* 23: 92-102. doi: 10.1016/j.gloenvcha.2012.07.005.

Brown, M. 2001. "Market Failures and Barriers as a Basis for Clean Energy Policies". *Energy Policy* 29 (14): 1197-1207.

Bulkeley, H., and M. Betsill. 2005. "Rethinking Sustainable Cities: Multilevel Governance and the Urban Politics of Climate Change". *Clean prod*. 14: pp. 42-63. doi: 10.1080/0964401042000310178.

Burton-Jones, A. 1999. *Knowledge Capitalism: Business, Work, and*

Learning in the New Economy. Oxford: Oxford University Press.
Carrillo-Hermosilla, J. Eco-innovation, http://www.eoearth.org/view/article/151923 (accessed 2015-11-23); 2012.
Castells, M. and Himanen P. 2002. *The Information Society and the Welfare State. The Finnish Model*. Oxford: Oxford University Press.
Chen, D. and Dahlman C. 2004. Knowledge and Development: A Cross-section Review. Policy Research Working Paper #3366. World Bank, Washington, DC.
Cheng, H., and Y. Hu. 2010. "Planning for sustainability in China's urban development: status and challenges for Dongtan eco-city project". J. Environ. Monit. 12:119-26. doi: 10.1039/b911473d.
Chong, W. T., M. S. Naghavi, S. C. Poh, T. M. I. Mahlia, and K. C. Pan. 2011. "Techno-economic analysis of a wind-solar hybrid renewable energy system with rainwater collection feature for urban high-rise application". *Appl. Energy* 88: 4067-77. doi: 10.1016/j.apenergy.2011.04.042.
Ciarreta, A., C. Gutiérrez-Hita, and S. Nasirov. 2011. "Renewable energy sources in the Spanish electricity market: Instruments and effects". *Renew. Sustain. Energy Rev*. 15: 2510-9. doi: 10.1016/j.rser.
Clark, C. W. 1973. "The economics of overexploitation". *Journal on Political Economy,* no. 181.
Coase, R. H. 1992. "The Institutional Structure of Production". *The American Economic Review* 82, no. 4: 713-719.
Coase, R. H. 1995. The problem of social cost. *Journal of Law and economics*. Oxford: Oxford University Press, no. 3: 1-44.
Colak, I., G. Fulli, S. Sagiroglu, M. Yesilbudak, and C. F. Covrig. 2015. "Smart grid projects in Europe: Current status, maturity and future scenarios". *Appl. Energy* 152: 58-70. doi: 10.1016/j.apenergy.2015.04.098.
Costanza R. and H. E. Daly. 1992. "Natural Capital and Sustainable Development". *Conservation Biology* 6, no. 1: 37-46.
Costanza R., R. de Groot, L. Braat, Ida Kubiszewski, L. Fioramonti, P. Sutton, S. Farber, and M. Grasso. 2017. "Twenty years of ecosystem services: How far have we come and how far do we still need to go". *Ecosystem Services* 28:1-16.
Cruz, M.R., D. Z. Fitiwi, S. F. Santos, and J. P. Catalão. 2018. "A comprehensive survey of flexibility options for supporting the low-carbon energy future". *Renewable and Sustainable Energy Reviews* 97: 338-53. doi: 10.1016/j. rser.2018.08.028.

Čiegis R. 2009. Economics of Natural Resources and the Environment. (in Lithuanian). Klaipėda: Klaipėda University Press.

Čiegis R. 2010. *Evaluation of sustainable development of industrial zones* (in Lithuanian). Šiauliai: Šiauliai University Press.

Čiegis, R. 2003. "Management Principles of Society's Sustainable Development and Transformation of the Economy". *Transformation in Business & Economics* 2, no. 2(4): 19-35.

Čiegis, R. 1997. *Sustainable economic development* (in Lithuanian). Kaunas: Vytautas: Magnus University Press.

Čiegis, R. 2002. *Sustainable development and the environment: an economic approach* (in Lithuanian). Vilnius: Aldorija.

Čiegis, R. 2004. *Economics and Environment: Managing Sustainable Development* (in Lithuanian). Kaunas: Vytautas Magnus University Press.

Čiegis, R., and E. Jasinskas. 2005. "Concepts of strong comparability versus concepts of strong and weak sustainability". *Engineering economics,* no. 5(45): 31-35.

Daly, H. E., and J. B. Cobb. 1994. *For the Common Good: Redirecting the Economy toward Community, the Environment, and a Sustainable Future.* (2nd updated and expanded ed.). Boston: Beacon Press.

Dar, G., B. C. Lin, and Y. Chen. 2015. "A circular economy model of economic growth". *Environmental modelling & software*, no. 73: 60-3. doi: 10.1016/j.envsoft.2015.06.014.

De Vries, B. J. M., D. P. van Vuuren, and M. M. Hoogwijk. 2007. "Renewable energy sources: Their global potential for the first-half of the 21st century at a global level: An integrated approach". *Energy Policy* 35: 259-287. doi: 10.1016/j.enpol.2006.09.002.

Degutis, A. 1998. *Individualism and Public Order* (in Lithuanian). Vilnius: Eugrimas.

Despres, Ch., and Chauvel, D. 2004. *Knowledge Horizons – The Present and the Promise of Knowledge Management.* Boston: Butterworth Heinemann.

Droege P, editor. 2008. *Urban Energy Transition*. Elsevier. doi:10.1016/B978-0-08-045341-5.00029-3.

Drucker, P. F. 2004. *Challenges of governance in the 21st century* (in Lithuanian). Vilnius: Tyto Alba.

Duer, H., and P. O. Christensen. 2010. "Socio-economic aspects of different biofuel development pathways". *Biomass and Bioenergy* 34: 237-43. doi: 10.1016/j.biombioe.2009.07.010.

Egenhofer, C. 2004. *Market-based options for security of energy supply.* Centre for European Policy Studies.

Eitan A., L. Herman, I. Fischhendler, G. Rosen. 2019. "Community–private sector partnerships in renewable energy". *Renewable and Sustainable Energy Reviews* 105, Part 1: 95-104. https://doi.org/10.1016/j.rser.2018.12.058.

Ellison, D., C. E. Morris, B. Locatelli, D. Sheil, J. Cohen, D. Murdiyarso, D. Gutierrez, et al. 2017. "Trees, forests and water: Cool insights for a hot world". *Global Environmental Change* 43: 51-61. https://doi.org/10.1016/j.gloenvcha.2017.01.002.

EURELECTRIC. 2004. Closing the circle of competitiveness: the need to reorient European electricity policy.

European Commission. 2009. Directive 2009/28/EC of the European Parliament and of the Council of 23 April 2009 on the promotion of the use of energy from renewable sources and amending and subsequently repealing Directives 2001/77/EC and 2003/30/EC. Official Journal of the European Communities, 5.6.2009, L 140/16.

European Commission. 2010. Directive 2010/75/EU of the European Parliament and of the Council of 24 November 2010 on industrial emissions (integrated pollution prevention and control). Official Journal of the European Communities, 17.12.2010, L 334/17.

European Commission. 2012. Directive 2012/27/EU of the European Parliament and of the Council of 25 October 2012 on energy efficiency, amending Directives 2009/125/EC and 2010/30/EU and repealing Directives 2004/8/EC and 2006//32/EC. Official Journal of the European Communities, 14.11.2012, L 315/1.

European Commission. 2014. State aid: Commission adopts new rules on public support for environmental protection and energy. Available on the internet: http://europa.eu/rapid/press-release_IP-14-400_en.htm.

European Commission. 2013. European Commission guidance for the design of renewable energy support schemes. Commission staff working document.

Ferng, J. J. 2002. "Toward a scenario analysis framework for energy footprints". *Ecological Economics*, no. 40: 53-69.

Figge, F., T. Hahn, S. Shaltegger, and M. Wagner. 2002. "The Sustainability Balanced Scorecard – Linking Sustainability Management to Business Strategy". *Business strategy and environment* 11(5): 269-284. doi: 10.1002/bse.339.

Folke, C., M. Hammer, R. Costanza, and A. Jansson. 1994. "Investing in natural capital—why and how". *Investing in Natural Capital: The Ecological Economics Approach to Sustainability*, edited by C. Folke, M. Hammer, R. Costanza and A Jansson. 1994, 1-20. Washington: D.C.

Friedman, M. 1998. *Capitalism and Freedom* (in Lithuanian). Vilnius: Mintis.
Fromm, E. 2008. *Escape from Freedom* (in Lithuanian). Vilnius: Verba Vera.
Geissdoerfer M., P. Savaget, N. M. P. Bocken and E. J. Hultink. 2017. "The Circular Economy – A new sustainability paradigm?" *Journal of Cleaner Production* 143: 757-768. https://doi.org/10.1016/j.jclepro.2016.12.048.
Geng Y., J. Fu, J. Sarkis, and B. Xue. 2011. "Towards a national circular economy indicator system in China: an evaluation and critical analysis". *J. Clean. Prod.*, no. 23: 216-24. doi: 10.1016/j.jclepro.2011.07.005.
Gilpin, R. 1998. *The Political Economy of International Relations* (in Lithuanian). Vilnius: Algarvė.
Griffin, J. M. and H. B. Steele. 1986. *Energy economics and policy.* Orlando, San Diego, San Francisco, New York, London, Toronto, Montreal, Sydney, Tokyo: Academic Press College Division.
Yadav, G., S. K. Mangla, S. Luthra, and G. P. Rai. 2019. "Developing a sustainable smart city framework for developing economies: An Indian context". *Sustainable Cities and Society*. 47, no. 10.
Guohui, S., and L. Yunfeng. 2012. "The Effect of Reinforcing the Concept of Circular Economy in West China Environmental Protection and Economic Development". *Procedia Environ. Sci.*, no. 12: 785-92. doi: 10.1016/j.proenv.2012.01.349.
Haberl, H, K. H. Erb, and F. Krausmann. 2001. "How to calculate and interpret ecological footprints for long periods of time: the case of Austria 1926-1995". *Ecological Economics*, 38: 25-45.
Hayek, F. A. von. 1967. *Prices and Production*. New York: Augustus M Kelley Pubs, 2nd Rev. edition.
Hansen, K., B. V. Mathiesen, and I. R. Skov. 2019. "Full energy system transition towards 100% renewable energy in Germany in 2050". *Renewable and Sustainable Energy Reviews* 102: 1-13. https://doi.org/10.1016/j.rser.2018.11.038.
Hargreaves, A. 2003. *Teaching in the Knowledge Society. Education in the Age of Insecurity*. New York: Teachers College Press.
Hargreaves, A. and Goodson I. 2006. "Educational Change over Time? The sustainability and non-sustainability of three decades of secondary school change and continuity". *Educational Administration Quarterly* 42 (1): 3-41.
Harmaajärvi, I. 2000. "EcoBalance model for assessing sustainability in residential areas and relevant case studies in Finland". *Environ. Impact Assess Rev.*, no 20: 373-80. doi: 10.1016/S0195-9255(00)00048-2.

Henderson, H. 2006. *Ethical markets: growing the green*. Chelsea Green Publishing.

Hicks, J. R. 1988. "The Foundations of Welfare Economics". *The Economic Journal* 49, no. 196: 696-712.

Hofierka J., and J. Kaňuk. 2009. "Assessment of photovoltaic potential in urban areas using open-source solar radiation tools". *Renew. Energy* 34: 2206-14. doi: 10.1016/j.renene.2009.02.021.

Holden, E. 2007. *Achieving Sustainable Mobility: Everyday and Leisure-time Travel in the EU*. Aldershot: Ashgate.

Holden, E., and K. Linnerud. 2007. "The sustainable development area: satisfying basic needs and safeguarding ecological sustainability". *Sust. Dev.* 15 (3): 174-187.

Hong, S. K. 2011. "Island ecology on biological-cultural diversities and human adaptation in seascapes". *Journal of Ecology and Field Biology* 33(2): 115-120. doi: 10.5141/JEFB.2010.33.2.115.

Hopwood, B., M. Mellor, and G. O'Brien. 2005. "Sustainable development: mapping different approaches". *Sust. Dev.* 13: 38-52.

Hotteling, H. 1931. "The economics of exhaustible resources". *Journal of Political Economy*, no. 39: 137-175.

Hu, D., and R. Wang. 1998. "Exploring eco-construction for local sustainability: An eco-village case study in China". *Ecol. Eng.*, no. 11:167-76. doi: 10.1016/S0925-8574(98)00032-9.

Hubbert, M. K. 1992. "Exponential growth as a transient phenomenon in human history". In *Valuing the Earth, economics, ecology, ethics*, edited by H. Daly and K. Townsend. Cambridge: Cambridge University Press.

Hudson, R. 2011. "From knowledge-based economy to ... knowledge-based economy? Reflections on changes in the economy and development policies in the North East of England". *Reg Stud* 45: 997-1012. doi:10.1080/00343400802662633.

Jackson, T. 2009. Prosperity without growing. The transition to a sustainable economy. Earthscan Ltd.: Sustainable development commission.

Jenniches, S. and E. Worrel. 2019. Regional economic and environmental impacts of renewable energy developments: Solar PV in the Aachen Region. *Energy for Sustainable Development* 48: 11-24. https://doi.org/10.1016/j.esd.2018.10.004.

Juknys, R. 2005. *Investigation of the Environment* (in Lithuanian). Kaunas: Vytautas Magnus University Press.

Jung, C. G. 1999. *Psychoanalysis and Philosophy* (in Lithuanian). *Rinktinė*. Vilnius: Pradai.

Kalenda C. 2007. *Ecological ethics* (in Lithuanian). Vilnius: Rosma.

Keynes, J. M. 1964. *The* general *theory of employment, interest*. New York: St Martin's Press.

Kilinc-Ata N. 2016. "The evaluation of renewable energy policies across EU countries and US states: An econometric approach". *Energy for Sustainable Development* 31: 83-90. https://doi.org/10.1016/j.esd.2015.12.006.

Kitzes, J. W. 2008. "Shrink and share: humanity's present and future ecological footprint". *Biological Science* 363: 467-475.

Klevas, V. 2010. "Regional approach for policies and measures aiming to sustainable energy development". In *Path to sustainable energy*, edited by J. Nathvani A. V. Ng. Rijeka: InTech.

Klevas, V., and M. Antinucci. 2004. "Integration of national and regional energy development programs in the Baltic States". *Energy policy* 32, no.3: 345-355.

Klevas, V. 2012. "Analysis of support assumptions and measures for promotion of renewable energy sources demand in regional aspect". In *Advances in energy research,* edited by M. J. Acosta, 99-122. New York: Nova Science Publishers.

Klevas V., K. Biekša and L. Murauskaitė. 2014. "Innovative method of RES integration into the regional energy development scenarios". *Energy Policy*, no. 64: 324-36. doi: 10.1016/j.enpol.2013.08.088.

Klevas, V. 1998. *Introduction to Public Energy Conservation Policy* (in Lithuanian). Kaunas: Energetika.

Klevas, V. 2015. *Justification of long-term economic policy of renewable energy sources*. New York: Nova Science Publishers.

Klevienė A. 2011. "Developing the structure of the knowledge economy in the field of sustainable energy" (in Lithuanian). *Applied Economics: Systematic Research* 5, no. 1: 131-143.

Klevienė, A., L. Murauskaitė, and V. Klevas. 2017. "Analysis of Municipal Knowledge Formation as an Example of Wide Use of Renewable Energy Sources" (in Lithuanian). (*Applied Economics: Systematic Research* 11, no. 1: 107-125. http://dx.doi.org/10.7220/AESR.2335.8742.2017.11.1.7.

Krautkraemer, J. A. 1988. "The rate of discount and the preservation of natural environments". *Natural resource modelling*, no. 2: 421-437.

Krugman, P. 1996. "Making Sense of the Competitiveness Debate". *Oxford Review of Economic Policy*, no. 12(3): 17-25.

Kuhn, T. S. 1970. *The Structure of Scientific Revolutions*. Chicago: University of Chicago Press. (2nd ed.).

Lafferty, W. M. 2004. *Governance for Sustainable Development. The Challenge of Adapting Form to Function.* Cheltenham: Elgar.

Lee, D., and D. Orr. 1975. "The private discount rate and resources conservation". *Can. J.Econ*, no 8: 351-356.

Lietuvos Rytas. 2018. Scientists break the myth of biofuels and say that EU can make a fatal mistake. 2018 02 09. Technologijos.lt. www.lrytas.lt.

Lithuanian Republic Ministry of Agriculture. Rules of funding for the production of biofuel // http://www3.lrs.lt/pls/inter3/dokpaieska.showdoc_l?p_id=325586&p_query=&p_tr2=. 2008.

Liu, W., X. Zhang, and S. Feng. 2019. "Does renewable energy policy work? Evidence from a panel data analysis". (2018) *Renewable Energy*. 135: 635-642. https://doi.org/10.1016/j.renene.2018.12.037.

Lockwood, B. 1997. Energy Security, Unpublished report from the ExternE Core Project (1996-1997) for European Commission DGXII, contract number JOS3-CT95-0002 EC 2002.

Maceina, A. 2004. *Nature and culture* (in Lithuanian). Vilnius: Margi raštai.

Mansfield, E. 1979. *Microeconomics*. New York, London: Norton Company.

Marckmann, B., K. Gram-Hanssen, and T. H. Christensen. 2012. "Sustainable Living and Co-Housing: Evidence from a Case Study of Eco-Villages". *Built. Environ.* 38: 413-29. doi: 10.2148/benv.38.3.413.

Marques, A. C., Fuinhas, J. A., and J. R. Pires-Manso. 2010. "Motivations driving renewable energy in European countries: A panel data approach". *Energy Policy* 38: 6877-85. doi: 10.1016/j. enpol.2010.07.003.

Marshall, A. 1961. *Principles of economics*. New York, London: Macmillan for the Royal Economic Society, (originally 1921).

Maslow, A. H. 2012. *Psychology of being* (in Lithuanian). Vilnius: Vaga.

McDonough, W., M. Braungart, P. T. Anastas, and J. B. Zimmerman. 2003. "Applying the Principles of Green Engineering to Cradle-to-Cradle Design". *Environ. Sci. Technol.*, no. 37: 434A-441A. doi: 10.1021/es0326322.

McKendrick, N., J. Brewer and J. H. Plumb. 1982. *The Birth of a Consumer Society*. London: Europa.

Meadowcroft, J. 2007. "National Sustainable Development Strategies: Features, Challenges and Reflexivity". *Environment* 17(3): 152-163.

Meadows, D. H., D. L. Meadows and J. Randers. 1992. Beyond the limits: global collapse or a sustainable future. Earthscan Publications.

Meyers, N. 1993. *Ultimate security: the environmental basis of political stability*. New York: Norton.

Mitsch W. H., Jorgenson S. E., eds. 1989. Ecological Engineering: An Introduction to Ecotechnology. New York.

Moran, D. W. 2008. "Measuring sustainable development — Nation by nation". *Ecological Economics* 64: 470-474.

Nordic Council of Ministers. 2019. *Nordic green to scale for cities and communities*.

Norgaard R. 1984. "Coevolutionary development potential" *Economics*, no. 60: 160-173.

Norgaard, J. S. 2001. Sustainable energy future-Nordic perspective. Keynote at Pan-European NGO Sustainable energy seminar, Denmark.

Nureev R. M. 2000. *Microeconomics course* (in Russian). Moscow: Norma Infra.

OECD. 2000. *Knowledge Management in the Learning Society*. Paris: OECD.

Ortega y Gasset, Ch. 1993. *The rebellion of mass* (in Lithuanian). Vilnius: Mintis.

Ostergaard, P. A. and Lund, H. 2010. "Climate Change Mitigation from a Bottom-up Community Approach". In *Sustainable communities design handbook*, edited by Woodrow W. Clark. USA: Butterworth – Heineman. https://doi.org/10.1016/B978-1-85617-804-4.00014-8.

Palojarvi A. P. 2013. *Experiences with ecological technologies and practices*. Vilnius: BMK Press.

Panwar N. L., S. C. Kaushik and S. Kothari. 2011. "Role of renewable energy sources in environmental protection: A review". *Renew. Sustain. Energy Rev*. 15: 1513-24. doi: 10.1016/j.rser.2010.11.037.

Paulauskas. S. 1999. *The dialectic of self-government*. Klaipeda: Klaipeda University Press.

Pearce, D. W., A. Markandya and E. B. Barbier. 1989. *Blueprint for a green economy*. London: Earthscan.

Pezzey, J. 1992. *Sustainable development concepts. An economic analysis*. Washington: World Bank Environment Paper, no 2.

Pigou, A. C. 1932. *The Economics of Welfare*. London: Macmillan and Co. 4th ed.

Popper, K. R. 1959. *The logic of scientific discovery*. London: Hutchinson and co.

Rae, C., and F. Bradley. 2012. "Energy autonomy in sustainable communities: A review of key issues". *Renew Sustain Energy Rev*. 16: 6497-506. doi:10.1016/j. rser.2012.08.002.

Rakštytė-Hoimian, J. 2019. Circular Economy: Use, Sort, Recycle, Repeat. Lithuanian Innovation Center; ELTA.

Redclift, M. 2005. "Sustainable development (1987-2005): an oxymoron comes of age". *Sus. Dev*. 13: 212-227.

Rees E. 2000. "Eco-footprint analysis: merits and brickbat". *Ecological Economics*, no. 32: 371-374.

Rifkin, J. 2012. *The Third Industrial Revolution* (in Lithuanian). Vilnius: Eugrimas.

Robe, K. H. 2002. "Strategic sustainable development – selection, design and synergies of applied tools". *Journal of Cleaner Production* 10:197-214.

Romer, P. M. 1986. "Increasing returns and long-run growth". *Journal of Political Economy.* 94: 1002-1037.

Romer, P. M. 1990. "Endogenous technological change". *Journal of Political Economy.* 98: 71-102.

Routti J., and P. Yla-Anttila. 2005. *Finland as a Knowledge Economy. Elements of Success and lesson learned.* World Bank. Washington: DC.

Sagoff, M. 1997. "Can we put a price on nature services?". *Philosophy and Public Policy*, no. 17: 8-12.

Sahlberg, P. (2004). Teaching and globalization. *International Research Journal of Managing Global Transitions* 2(1): 65-83.

Sahlberg, P. 2006. "Education Reform for Raising Economic Competitiveness" *Journal of Educational Change* 7, no. 4: 259-287.

Samuelson, P. A. 1983. Enlarged ed. *Foundations of Economic Analysis.* Harvard: Harvard University Press.

Santolini L., F. Mancini, and D. A. Garcia. 2019. "A GIS-based model to assess electric energy consumptions and usable renewable energy potential in Lazio region at municipality scale". *Sustainable Cities and Society* 46. https://doi.org/10.1016/j.scs.2018.12.041.

Schelling, F. W. J. 1995. *Philosophy of Human Freedom* (in Lithuanian). Vilnius: Pradai.

Schopenhauer, A. 2001. *Parerga and Paralipomena* (in Lithuanian). Vilnius: Pradai.

Schumpeter, J. A. 1994. *The theory of economic development: an inquiry into profits.* Oxford: Oxford University Press.

Schumpeter, J. A. 2014. *Capitalism, socialism and democracy* (2nd ed.). Virginia: Floyd.

Shen, Y. C., G. T. Lin, K. P Li, and B. J. Yuan. 2010. "An assessment of exploiting renewable energy sources with concerns of policy and technology". *Energy Policy* 38: 4604-16. doi: 10.1016/j. enpol.2010.04.016.

Shiva V., "The greening of global reach". 1992. *The Ecologist* 22: 327-328.

Smith, A. 1999. The Wealth of Nations: Books I-III. London: Penguin Books.

Snitka, V. 2002. *Research, technology, innovation policy and knowledge economy development. Dimensions of the National Plan* (in Lithuanian). Kaunas: Naujasis Lankas.

Solow, R. M. 1956. "A contribution to the theory of economic growth". *Quar. J. Econ*, no. 70: 65-94.

Solow, R.M. 1974. "Intergenerational equity and exhaustible resources". *Rev. Econ. Stud.* 41: 29-45. doi: 10.2307/2296370.

Sonenblum, S. 1978 *The energy connections: between energy and economy*. Cambridge: Ballinger Publishing Company.

Strange, S. 1998. *State and Markets* (in Lithuanian). Vilnius: Eugrimas.

Strantzali E., and K. Aravossis. 2016. "Decision making in renewable energy investments: A review". *Renew. Sustain. Energy. Rev.* 55: 885-98. doi: 10.1016/j.rser.2015.11.021.

Tahvonen, O and J. Kuuluvainen. 1993. "Economic growth, pollution and renewable resources". *J. Environ. Econ. Manage*, no. 24:101-118.

Takeuchi K., Y. Namiki, and H. Tanaka. 1998. "Designing eco-villages for revitalizing Japanese rural areas". *Ecol. Eng.* 11: 177-97. doi: 10.1016/S0925-8574(98)00031-7.

Teihlhard de Chardin, P. 1995. *The human phenomenon* (in Lithuanian). Vilnius: Mintis.

Thoreau H. D. 1985. *Walden or life in the woods* (in Lithuanian). Vilnius: Vaga.

Toffler, A. 2001. *Power change: knowledge, wealth and violence as the 21st century approaches*. (in Lithuanian). Vilnius: Tyto Alba.

Tzoulas K., K. Korpela, S. Venn, V. Yli-Pelkonen, V. Kaźmierczak, A, Niemela J, et al. 2007. "Promoting ecosystem and human health in urban areas using Green Infrastructure: A literature review". *Landsc. Urban Plan.* 81:167-78. doi: 10.1016/j.landurbplan.2007.02.001.

Van den Bergh, J., and F. Grazi. 2010. On the policy relevance of ecological footprints. *Environ. Sci. Technol.* 44: 4843-4844.

Van Dijk S., M. Tenpierik, van den A. Dobbelsteen. 2014. "Continuing the building's cycles: A literature review and analysis of current systems theories in comparison with the theory of Cradle to Cradle". *Resour. Conserv. Recycl.*, no. 82: 21-34. doi: 10.1016/j.resconrec.2013.10.007.

Vilpišauskas, R. 2004. "International Competitiveness and Lithuanian Export Policy". *Money Studies*, no. 1: 54-69.

Wackernagel M., L. Onisto, P. Bello, A. Callejas Linares, I. S. Lopez Falfa, J. Mendez Garcıa, A. I., and Suarez Guerrero. 1999. "National natural capital accounting with the ecological footprint concept". *Ecological Economics* 29, no 375: 90.

Wackernagel, M. 1999. "Ecological economic forum: Why sustainability analyses must include biophysical assessments". *Ecological Economics* 29: 13-15.

Wackernagel, M. and W. Rees. 1997. *Our ecological footprint: reducing human impact on the Earth*. Philadelphia: New society publishers.

Wang R., F. Li, D. Hu, and B. Li. 2011. "Understanding eco-complexity: Social-Economic-Natural Complex Ecosystem approach". *Ecol. Complex.*, no. 8: 15-29. doi: 10.1016/j.ecocom.2010.11.001.

Weber, M. 1997. Protestant ethics and the spirit of capitalism (in Lithuanian). Vilnius: Pradai.

Wu H., Y. Shi, Q. Xia, and W. Zhu. 2014. "Effectiveness of the policy of circular economy in China: A DEA-based analysis for the period of 11th five-year-plan". *Resour. Conserv. Recycl.*, no.83: 163-75. doi: 10.1016/j.resconrec.2013.10.003.

Zheng Y. Y., and S. Gao. 2013. "Exploration on the Eco-Village Planning from the Perspective of Low-Carbon". *Appl. Mech. Mater*. 357-360. doi: 10.4028/www.scientific.net/AMM.357-360.1945.

INDEX

D

E

I

K

L

M

N

O

P

Q

R

S